NETWORKING 101

Uyless

PRENTICE HALL PTR
UPPER SADDLE RIVER, NJ 07458
WWW.PHPTR.COM

ISBN 0-13-093126-8

90000

9 780130 931269

Library of Congress Cataloging-in-Publication Data

Black, Uyless D.
   Networking 101 / Uyless Black.
     p. cm.
   Includes index.
   ISBN 0-13-093126-8
    1. Computer networks. I. Title.

TK5105.5 .B56535 2001
004.6--dc21

2001033841

Editorial/production supervision: *Laura Burgess*
Cover design director: *Jerry Votta*
Cover design: *Design Source*
Acquisitions editor: *Mary Franz*
Marketing manager: *Dan DePasquale*
Editorial assistant: *Noreen Regina*
Manufacturing manager: *Alexis R. Heydt*

 © 2002 by Prentice Hall PTR
Prentice-Hall, Inc.
Upper Saddle River, NJ 07458

Prentice Hall books are widely used by corporations and government
agencies for training, marketing, and resale. The publisher offers
discounts on this book when ordered in bulk quantities.

For more information, contact:
Phone: 800-382-3419   Fax: 201-236-7141   e-mail: corpsales@prenhall.com
or write:
Corporate Sales Department, Prentice Hall PTR, One Lake Street, Upper Saddle River, NJ 07458

Printed in the United States of America
10 9 8 7 6 5 4 3 2 1

ISBN: 0-13-093126-8

Pearson Education LTD.
Pearson Education Australia PTY, Limited
Pearson Education Singapore, Pte. Ltd.
Pearson Education North Asia Ltd.
Pearson Education Canada, Ltd.
Pearson Educación de Mexico, S.A. de C.V.
Pearson Education — Japan
Pearson Education Malaysia, Pte. Ltd.
Pearson Education, Upper Saddle River, New Jersey

Dedication

This book is dedicated to my brothers
David, Ed, Ross, Jim, and Tom

Contents

Preface

In the past, some of my clients, and most of my friends and relatives, have asked me to write an introductory book on computer networks. These non-technical folks expressed a wish to read a book I wrote that they could actually understand. For my previous books, I told them to just look at the pictures, but that did more harm than good. So, for the networking-empaired, be you a client, friend, relative, or any combination thereof, this book is for you.

Joking aside, my intent in writing this book is to explain data networks and the Internet in nonengineering, nontechnical terms. Given this goal, it is impossible to describe a computer network without any technical jargon whatsoever. But I have been careful in the use of buzz-words, and have attempted to explain technical concepts in nontechnical terms.

The writing of this book has been a new experience for me. It is my first attempt at writing a beginner's book on the subject of computer networks. So, both of us are venturing into something new: myself in my writing, and you in reading this book.

There are two prerequisites to reading *Networking 101*. First, you should have logged on to the Internet or some other data network, maybe even successfully.

Second, you should be able to count up to 2. But the numbers are not 1 and 2; you must start at 0 and proceed to 1. If 0 is not a valid number in your mind, don't read any further.

If you have mastered these prerequisites, then welcome to the world of Networking 101.

I hope you learn a substantial amount from reading this book, and I hope you enjoy the process. I have interjected a few light comments here and there to "lighten the load" for the Networking 101 newcomer.

For the seasoned networking veteran, I trust I have presented some novel ways for you to think about computer networks.

Notes for the Reader

Approach to Describing User Network Sessions

Users can exchange information with each other through a computer network in a number of ways. One method is conventional email, another is in public chat rooms, another is private instant messaging, yet another is a Web browser, as well as a direct file transfer, and so on. All of the methods vary in how they support user communications.

To keep the explanations and examples in this introductory course reasonably simple, some of the components involved in these operations are "folded into" the user computer. That is, some examples show communications occurring between, say, two user computers, when other machines may be involved in the process. I considered providing examples of each communications process for each specific subject in this book, but I quickly realized the book would have to be two or three times its present size.

Appendix A reviews each of these various session scenarios. The text in the chapters refers often to this appendix and explains the similarities and differences where appropriate. For the beginner, Appendix A might be too detailed as a starter. But as we proceed through the chapters, I recommend specific parts of this appendix to study when appropriate.

Getting Started

This chapter begins our journey to solve the Networking 101 puzzle. We examine a few basic pieces of the puzzle, and we learn why computer networks are vital to our businesses and to many elements of our personal life. Like it or not, most aspects of our lives depend on these networks.

Several key attributes of computer networks are described, such as resource sharing and switching. Another important attribute is explained: the networks' ability to provide backup facilities to network customers, such that the customers are not denied their services, even when problems occur.

Computer Networks and Why They Exist

What is a computer network? The basic definition is simple. A computer network is the *connection* of multiple computers. The focus in this book is on wide area networks: those that may span cities and countries.

This definition of a computer network is indeed simple, except for one part of the definition. What is a connection? The next part of the chapter explains this term.

To get things started, I suggest you set up this experiment. As you go though your normal routine of daily activities, try getting through the day *without* using a computer network. If you are able to accomplish this feat, you cannot make any telephone calls; the ATM bank machines are off-limits; don't even think of trying to get a hotel or plane reservation. These systems use computer networks.

By the way, turn off the TV and the radio; they are built on computer networks. And while you are at it, turn off all your lights and other electrical appliances—they are also depend on computer networks.

You may be able to accomplish the experiment if you stay in bed, but not necessarily. It is likely the mattress on which you are reposing has been built with the aid of computers and computer networks. You can't stay in your home; it is designed and built with the help of computer networks.

With the failed experiment behind us, perhaps accompanied by a foreboding realization of our dependency on the computer and computer networks, we must move on.

To move on, two assumptions are made.

  ❏ Assumption one: computers are connected by *communications links*. As shown in Figure 1.1, these links are (say) telephone lines, furnished by companies such as AT&T, MCI, Sprint, and British Telecom.

  ❏ Assumption two: These *service providers* (so named because they provide a service to customers) are not constructing these facilities with altruistic intentions. The facilities cost a lot of money to build, and the service providers charge their customers for the use of these facilities. Therefore, the customer's *traffic* (such as telephone calls, email, etc.) is known as *payload* to these providers, because they view this traffic as just that: providing them revenue, that is, payload.

Example of a Computer Network

Figure 1.1 depicts a simple computer network, with only four machines connected together. These machines, also called network *nodes*, are labeled A, B, C, and D. They need not be conventional computers. They may also be workstations, palm devices, fax machines, telephones, and so on.

Figure 1.1   A Simple Computer Network

In this example, they are situated in various parts of the country. They could also be located inside a building, but they are still connected with some form of a communications link, such as a simple copper wire.

The Joys of Uptime

One of the attractive aspects of computer networks is that they can provide their users (customers) *uptime* (or *robustness*). For example, assume a customer's traffic, such as email or an instant chat room message (see Appendix A for a description of these types of user traffic) is being transported from computer A to computer D. The message is relayed through node C. Further assume that node C has problems or perhaps the link between A and C is inoperable because the wire that connects A and C was cut.[1] That being the case, of course, traffic cannot be sent between A and C.

---

1. The cutting of telephone wires is a common occurrence. At first glance, this inadvertent action seems absurd; after all, everyone should know where all those wires between customers and the telephone offices are buried. Yes, they should know, but these wires are "all over the place." Sometimes, a backhoe finds them.

Fortunately, a network is capable of diverting the customer's traffic to an alternate path. But be aware that your link to a network may not have this capability, because the link is a point-to-point connection to this network. Our example is in the network itself.

Why is uptime so important? Just imagine what would happen if the banking networks of the world could not continue operating because a backhoe cut a copper wire, the link between two major banks. Obviously, the break would disrupt the professional and personal lives of many people.

Therefore, most computer networks are capable of diverting the customers' traffic around problem areas. For example, if the traffic cannot be sent to site C from A, it can be diverted to site B, for final delivery to site D. In most situations, this diversion is never revealed to the network customers.

Point-to-Point Connections?

There is another reason for using computer networks. It is impossible to have direct, point-to-point communications links to all the parties in the world with whom we wish to exchange an email or engage in a telephone conversation. Let's see why.

The networking picture is changed slightly, as shown in Figure 1.2. The four computers are now *completely* connected together with communications links. In addition to the previous links, additional links exist between A and D and C and B. This arrangement is called a fully meshed, point-to-point network. A link, such as a telephone line of copper wire, connects each of these computers with the others.

This arrangement is impossible to implement with wires. To illustrate, a node in the northwest part of the United States is added to the network. This action results in the installation of links to all the other computers (see Figure 1.3). Next, another node is added in Florida (see Figure 1.4).

These continued additions of sites to the network won't work. A computer network cannot possibly have all these point-to-point connections (unless just a few machines are connected to each other). The earth would be laden with wires running between millions of computers!

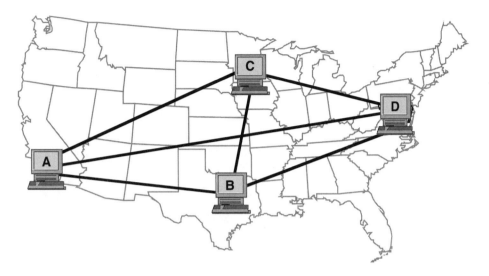

Figure 1.2 Point-to-Point Configuration

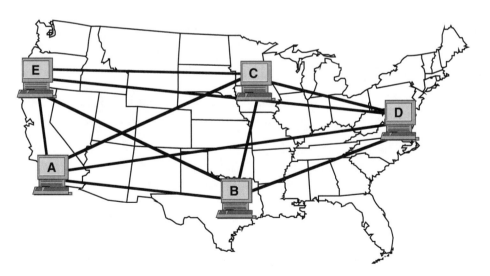

Figure 1.3 Adding a Node in the Northwest

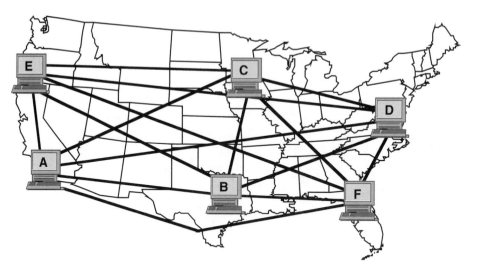

Figure 1.4   Adding Another Node in Florida

Consequently, another important reason for using computer networks is to reduce the number of physical connections (the links) that might exist between machines. How is this feat accomplished?

The Switch

Another machine is installed in the network. It is called the *switch*, and it is so named because it relays or switches traffic to various nodes in the network.[2]

The switch is placed in the picture, as shown in Figure 1.5. If traffic is sent between the computers (or telephones, for that matter), the point-to-point links are not needed. Rather, the customer's traffic is sent to the switch and the

---

2. Other terms are used to describe a switch. You may have heard the term router, for example, a prevalent term in computer networks. At this juncture, the term switch fits our needs just fine. Later, other terms are introduced, as appropriate.

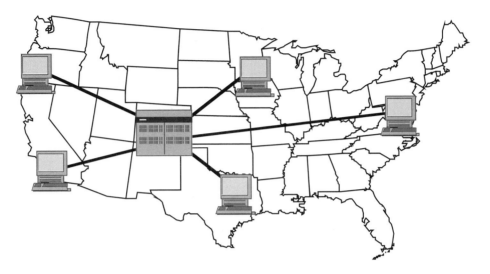

Figure 1.5   Adding a Switch to the Network

switch relays the traffic to the final recipient (the other customer). Thus, an immense amount of money is saved by reducing the number of communications links that are installed between computers, telephones, etc.

But it is not just about money. It is the common-sense realization that point-to-point connections cannot be physically achieved on a large scale wherein many computers or telephones must be connected together. Thus, switches are not an option. Computer networks (or for that matter, telephone networks) cannot exist without switches.

Resource Sharing

These discussions lead to another reason for the use of networks: *resource sharing*. This idea is illustrated by an example of the largest and perhaps most successful communications network in the world. No, it is not the Internet, it is the telephone network.

In Figure 1.6, the previous figure is changed slightly. The switch is now relaying a telephone call between two parties who are engaged in a conversation over the telephone network.

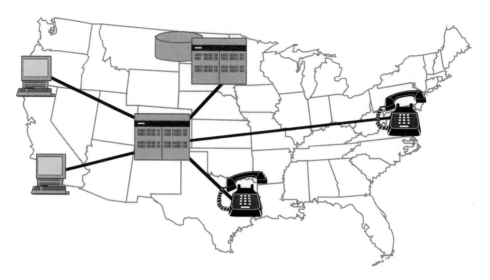

Figure 1.6   Using the Switch to Relay Telephone Calls

There is another component at the top of the map in Figure 1.6. It is another switch. Next to the switch is an icon that is used to denote disk storage. Stored on these disk files are databases that support applications such as the well-known 800, 900, 911 dialing services. The two telephone users in this figure have access to, for example, 800 toll-free call services. So do other telephone users, through the joint use of these databases. That is why the term *resource sharing* is used: these databases are a shared resource.

These files and their information are taken for granted. Yet through the use of computer networks, network customers have at their fingertips the services of toll-free dialing, emergency services, call forwarding, do not disturb, and many other service features. So, again, sharing data is another example of one of the reasons for using computer networks.

Examples of Network Services

This part of the chapter provides a few more examples of how networks allow network users to access and possibly share data, as depicted in Figure 1.7. Many of us log on to networks, perhaps even the Internet, and access shared

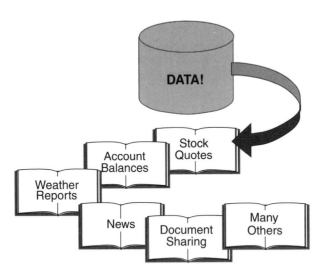

Figure 1.7 Examples of Network Services

files to view stock quotes.[3] We often log onto networks to find our account balances at stores or credit card firms (one hopes these files are not shared). We have shared access to weather reports, the news reports, and so on.

Through the use of networks, I can activate document-sharing activities with my colleagues on a personal, interactive basis. As an example, I often log on to the Internet and download documents (like a spreadsheet or a drawing) to members of one of my project teams. My colleagues and I can jointly participate in manipulating the spreadsheet or jointly contribute to the drawing.

It is a wonderful resource, and we do not have to board a plane to fly to a meeting in order to collaborate in this work. We do it all through computer networks. It is an understatement to say that we save an immense amount of money, misery, and time by using the Internet for this work, instead of the airlines' networks.

---

3. The Internet is a computer network discussed in considerable detail later.

A Network by Any Other Name…

Many different kinds of networks are in operation today. Some are called local area networks. Some are called wide area networks. You may have heard of the term Ethernet, which is an example of a local area network. You may have heard of Frame Relay, or ATM (Asynchronous Transfer Mode). These networks are examples of wide area networks.

We need not concern ourselves with those specific network technologies in Networking 101. What we want to understand is that all these networks have a common goal: to support the transport of information between their users, you and me.

They are marvelous inventions. Now let's find out how they operate in the next chapters.

Summary

We might succeed in our experiment of avoiding the use of computer networks for the one-day trial if we made one simple decision: find a cave and spend the day there. If hungry or thirsty, we will have to eat raw and newly picked berries and drink spring water. Most of our nutritional intakes in this modern world are made with the aid of computer networks.

We must walk to the cave, because an automobile has scores of networks operating under its hood; so do trains, so do airplanes (computer networks are used in the design of roller blades and bicycles, not to mention the sneaker that goes "boing, boing").

The realization of our dependence on computer networks, on machines for that matter, might invoke feelings of exhilaration or despair. We might also view a glass of water as half-full or half-empty. It depends on our perspective.

A computer network is a tool, an instrument. It is not unlike a hammer. We use a hammer for our own purposes; so too should we use computers and computer networks.

Regardless of our feelings about computer networks, glasses of water, or life in general, computer networks are so deeply interwoven into the fabric of our everyday lives that we cannot function as a coherent and prosperous society without them.

Yes, all true. But a caveat is in order. It deals with how these networks, these *instruments*, are used. Many years ago, I read about an idea that sticks in my mind as the *law of the instrument*. It is exemplified by a child who picks up a hammer and looks for something to pound. The mark of intelligence in regard to our subject of computers and computer networks is knowing not only how to *create* an instrument, but how to *use* it.

Chapter 2

Computer and Human Communications

This chapter expands our efforts to piece together the networking 101 puzzle. In so doing, we begin by examining how computers communicate with each other through networks, and we compare this process with human communications. I am not suggesting computers can talk as we humans do, but we will see that they exhibit traits similar to our everyday discourses with each other.

I introduce the concept of *codes*, a method of representing computer "languages," and we learn how codes enable computers to communicate with each other.

The last part of the chapter shows some examples of computer dialogues, and compares them to similar dialogues between humans. These dialogues between humans are called *conversations*; between computers, they are called *protocols*.

Communications Between Humans

Like humans, computers and computer networks have a method for communicating, for exchanging information. For humans, the method is a language

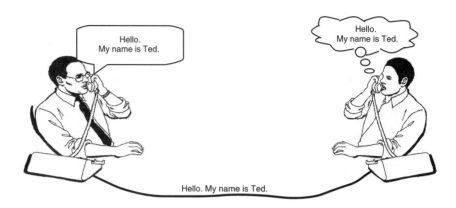

Figure 2.1　Communications Between Humans

to support our communications. In Figure 2.1, Ted speaks over the telephone network to another person, say, Bob, and he says, "Hello. My name is Ted." The right side of Figure 2.1 shows that Bob hears Ted's oral message. Bob records this message in his mind, perhaps for future use. Or perhaps Bob ignores Ted's message for any number of human reasons.

Several actions occur when oral communications take place over the telephone network. The telephone accepts Ted's acoustical speech (a sound wave) and transforms it into an electrical signal (an electrical wave). The electrical speech is then sent over the telephone network to the receiving telephone set, where the electrical speech is transformed back to the acoustical speech signal for Bob to hear.

Communications Between Computers

Computers also have a "language" for exchanging information with each other. This language is not the spoken word as in Ted and Bob's oral communications. In spite of what some people claim, the computer can't talk, it can only mimic talk. Ted's spoken word is translated into other representations.

One example is a written representation of Ted's salutation to Bob, say, in the form of email or in an instant message in a chat room (see Appendix A for information on these user session scenarios). To affect this operation, Ted

Figure 2.2   Communications Between Computers

types words (data) into his computer and sends the words to Bob's computer, or Bob's server.

In computer networks, the "Hello. My name is Ted." is conveyed by electronic (or optical) representations, rather than by an oral, audio signal. These representations are called codes, and they are explained shortly.

In the example in Figure 2.2, Ted is entering this message on his computer keyboard. The message is sent to Bob, where it is displayed on his computer screen.

Figure 2.2 also shows that Ted may be talking to Bob on the telephone at the same time he is entering data on this computer keyboard. If this arrangement is provided, Ted is likely typing in information other than the hello. After all, Ted has already said hello to Bob through the telephone. For example, Ted may be entering a spreadsheet of accounting information to send to Bob for them to discuss over the telephone.

We can now explore how the computers communicate with each other through a network; that is, how they send Ted's message to Bob.

Codes: The Language of Computer Networks

Earlier, we touched on an analogy between humans and the computer. It is the use of *languages* to convey the intelligence, the meaning of the dialogue. For humans, the language may be Arabic, English, Spanish, and so on. For computers, the languages are called codes.

It's a Matter of 1s and 0s

How are these codes represented in computer networks? They are represented as the numbers 1 and 0. The idea is simple: set up strings of 1s and 0s in various, specific combinations to represent the words and sentences of the machine's language. Let's take a look at some examples of these codes and learn what they mean.

Goodbye or End of Transmission

The code of 0010000 means EOT, for end of transmission (a start of transmission or hello is explained next).[1] This string of 1s and 0s is sent from one machine to another to say "goodbye." This process takes place just after you direct your PC or workstation to "stop run," "log-off," "sign off," or some other command you give to your computer.

Let's think about this process. You inform your computer you want to stop communicating with, say, a chat partner on the Internet. Fine, but since you are logged on to the Net (as the Internet is called), your computer is also communicating with your chat partner's computer. Your computer must accept your "goodbye" command and send the computer's goodbye EOT code to the computer of your chatting partner. After all, you can't just turn off your computer and leave your partner sitting at their computer waiting for your next pearl of wisdom.

Consequently, as seen in Figure 2.3, in event 1, Bob enters "sign off" (or clicks on the sign off button on the computer screen). In event 2, Bob's computer obeys Bob's directive and sends the EOT code to Ted's computer. Ted's computer accepts and displays the information on its screen (event 3). Ted now has sufficient information that he too can log off and turn off his

---

1. Appendix C of this book contains a table of codes. Several of the codes in this table are used in several chapters in this book. The curious reader may wish to peruse this table and the accompanying tutorial.

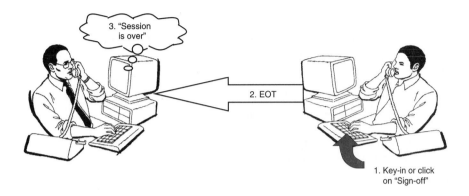

Figure 2.3 Example of "Saying Goodbye"

machine. In this manner, all parties know that the chat session is over; Ted and Bob know it, and so do their computers.

Private Instant Messaging, Chat Rooms, and Email

The example thus far shows the support of a private messaging session between two users. This operation requires fast response from the network, since Ted and Bob are sitting at their terminals sending traffic to each other and waiting for each other's responses. Thus, this operation requires *instant messaging*.

Ted and Bob can also communicate with each other (and other people) with another form of instant messaging called a chat room. The main difference between the chat room and the instant messaging described in the previous paragraph is that the chat room is public and instant messaging is private.

For clarification, instant messaging comes in two forms: public (chat rooms) and private. Even this "clarification" can become a bit murky, because some video conference applications support a private chat room, which is set up only for the conference participants. But within this private chat room, the individual participants can choose to communicate with each other through private or public chat rooms. For more information on these systems, take a look at scenarios 1, 2, and 3 in Appendix A.

If either party (Ted or Bob) is not logged-on to the network, the traffic transfer is still supported. In this situation, Ted sends a message to Bob, but the messages are stored at another machine in the network, called a *mail server*. Ted's email goes first to a designated mail server. Later, Bob can log on to the network, and get Ted's email that is stored at this server. Scenario 4 in Appendix A explains this type of service.

Systems are being developed that do not require the use of an intervening server. In effect, the server capabilities are pared down and placed in the user's computer. Many of the examples in this book use this scenario.

What About Hello?

You are likely thinking that I am getting the goodbye wagon ahead of the hello horse. I am, but I introduced the goodbye before the hello because the computer code of EOT is somewhat self-descriptive; that is, "end of transmission" means just that.

The hello is a bit more cryptic, and various computers and computer networks use different codes of 1s and 0s to represent the hello. One code that is used in many systems is called the "SYN" (pronounced sin, and not nearly as intriguing as it sounds). The term means synchronization. The string of 1s and 0s to represent this code is 0110100. This idea is shown in Figure 2.4.

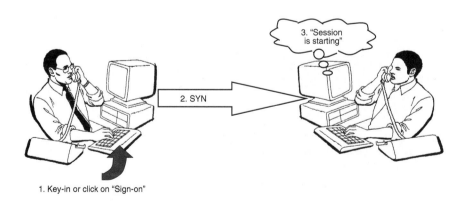

Figure 2.4 Example of "Saying Hello": the Cryptic SYN

Just About Everything Needs Synchronization

Many things encountered in everyday life use some form of synchronization. In our previous example, a telephone ringing signal at Bob's telephone is also a form of synchronization. The ring alerts Bob (gets his attention) to the fact that someone wants to talk to him. In the computer world, a SYN code is used to get the computer's attention.

As noted, one form of synchronization for humans is our common hello. It too alerts the listener and gets his or her attention. And if I may play on words regarding another form of human communications: engaging in a little bit of sin often requires some preliminary SYN to take place between the two communicating parties.

Anyway, the human hello idea is the same as a computer hello, which is in the form of a set of 1s and 0s. Don't make it any more complicated, because it isn't! In almost all aspects of our lives, some form of synchronization is needed for humans to live beyond chaos. Computers and computer networks are no different in this regard.

Why the Cryptic SYN?

You are probably asking: Why can't the computer simply send out the 1s and 0s of our salutation and have the message called a simple "hello" and not a cryptic notation like SYN? For that matter, why can't the SYN be abbreviated to something like HEL? Therefore, why can't the SYN bits of 0110100 be called HEL, for hello?

In effect, that is exactly what is happening: these strings of 1s and 0s actually represent the computer's way of greeting another computer.

The computer can indeed use a less obscure notation for a common hello. But several years ago, some computer communications designers chose to use seemingly obscure notations for special reasons (perhaps to make their trade seem a bit more exotic).

The fact remains that SYN has long been used to convey the idea of the hello, which certainly conveys the idea of an initial "synchronization" between the communicating parties. So, the code SYN is a logical and shortened form for synchronization. It could just as easily be something else, but it isn't: SYN is the computer's way (one way) of saying hello to another computer.

To summarize, the SYN does the same thing in computer networks that we humans do in our daily communications. In many computer networks (for example, the Internet), the SYN code is used by a computer to say hello and get the attention of the receiving computer (Bob's).[2] The idea is for the computers to get themselves synchronized first and then allow the computer users to get their own synchronization established between each other, say, in the form of email or chat messages.

Therefore, we can modify our example slightly to explain that a SYN message is exchanged between computers *before* Ted actually sends his email or chat message to Bob.

Codes: We've Been Using Them for Centuries

Humans have been using codes for many years. In earlier days, codes were a form of encryption, typically substituting one letter in the alphabet for another, in order to confuse a third party who might be trying to read the message. This process was known only to the sender and the receiver, so they could exchange secrets.

Those codes are not the ones that interest us here; indeed, we want our codes to clarify, not obscure, communications. In addition, we want to learn about how computers and computer networks operate, so we need to concentrate on machine codes and not human cipher codes.

---

2. It is likely some of the readers of this text are at Networking 102 or 103 levels. For those readers, I will provide an occasional footnote for your edification. The Networking 101 readers can ignore these footnotes and not suffer any ill effects. In fact, I do not recommend these footnotes for you Networking 101 readers unless you are somewhat technically masochistic. For the first footnote: The SYN (that is, the hello) is actually used by an Internet software program in the computer called the Transmission Control Protocol (TCP), although some older systems used the SYN code for other protocols.

The Morse Code

The most basic machine code, the one first used to transmit electronic information on a mass scale, was the Morse code, used on telegraphs. The telegraph is credited as the foundation of many of the data communications concepts that are in use today, many of which are explained in this book.

In about 1832, Samuel F. B. Morse began work on the development of the first telegraph. During this endeavor, he and Alfred Vail designed a code in 1838 to represent the letters of the alphabet with specific sequences of electrical current on the telegraph link. These signals were strung together to form letters and numbers by this procedure:

❐ Space: absence of an electric current

❐ Dot: an electric current of short duration

❐ Dash: an electric current of longer duration—three times longer than a dot

One of the codes that many of us know from old movies was the emergency code of SOS. It was sent as: dot, dot, dot, dash, dash, dash, dot, dot, dot.

■ Common Sense in Action

The Morse code was cleverly designed. The most frequently occurring characters were assigned short code symbols. For example, the frequently used letter E was assigned the symbol value of one dot. The seldom-used letter Z was assigned successive dash, dash, dot, dot symbols. This variable-length code reduced the number of strokes the operator had to make and also decreased the number of signals transmitted across the telegraph link.

How did these brilliant ideas come about? By common sense. Morse and Vail paid a visit to a newspaper office. They determined the Morse code by counting the number of letters in the bins of a printer's character type box of As, Bs, Cs, and so on. Modern information theory tells us the efficiency of Morse code, over 150 years old, can only be improved by some 15 percent.

Binary Numbers: Bits, Bytes, Nibbles, and, Sometimes, Octets

Each 1 or 0 is called a *bit*. A group of eight bits makes up a *byte* or *octet* (although in many systems seven bits make up a byte). In the 1960s IBM coined the term *byte* to describe the 8-bit codes and numbers used in its famous System/360 computer family. Due to IBM's prominence in those days, the term byte became a common word. However, the "other" international standards organizations chose the term octet instead of byte.

Sometimes, network personnel must deal with only parts of a byte, that is, a select few of the bits. These bits of the full byte are called *nibbles*. The origin of this term in relation to byte is obvious.

Binary numbers and codes are represented by several signaling techniques. The data can be represented simply by a current being turned on or off (as in the old telegraph). It is also possible to use the voltage state of the line (such as on/off voltage or positive or negative voltage) to represent 1s and 0s. Increasingly, optical fiber systems are used to transmit light pulses (light is present or it is not present) to represent 1s and 0s.

The 1s and 0s are also strung together to form codes like EOT. Here is an example in Figure 2.5. Recall that EOT is made up of a 7-bit binary string of 001000.[3]

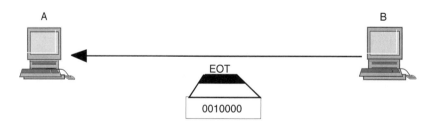

Figure 2.5   Another Example of the EOT Code

---

3. Figure 2.5 shows the order of the bits sent on the link as 0010000. Some systems reverse this order and send 0000100. Obviously, the machines that send and receive traffic to and from each other must know which order is being used. It's something like humans agreeing on a common language (Spanish, French, etc.) Some computers are "smart" enough to examine the bits as they are coming into the machine and make decisions about the specific code and the ordering of the bits in the code.

Extending the Analogy

It will prove helpful to extend the analogy of human and computer communications and show more examples of how computers and computer networks use human communications concepts to communicate with each other. These examples are not exhaustive. Table 2.1 lists the protocol dialogues illustrated in Figure 2.6.

Table 2.1   Protocol Dialogue Examples

Function	Human-to-human	Machine-to-machine
Invitation to communicate	"Talk to me"	A poll message ("DC1" code)
Invitation to communicate	"I want to talk to you"	A select message ("DC2" code)
Comprehending the communications	"I understand"	An "ACK" code
Not comprehending the communications	"I don't understand"	A "NAK" code

Note: "DC" indicates (a) device control or (b) data communications control.

The codes can be combined (by use of more than one code) to create many elaborate "conversations" between machines. Later in this book, we examine some more possibilities.

The Path Between the Computers

The traffic sent between computers on the communications link is conveyed in one of two ways: (a) on a wire or (b) in the air. The first link type is called wire-based, and the second type is called wireless.

Figure 2.7 shows some prominent examples of both wire-based and wireless communications paths.

 ❑ Copper-pair: This medium is the wire used by telephones. The wire connects our phones to the telephone company's Central Office (CO). At this office, the wires are terminated and usually then fed into another medium such as optical fiber.

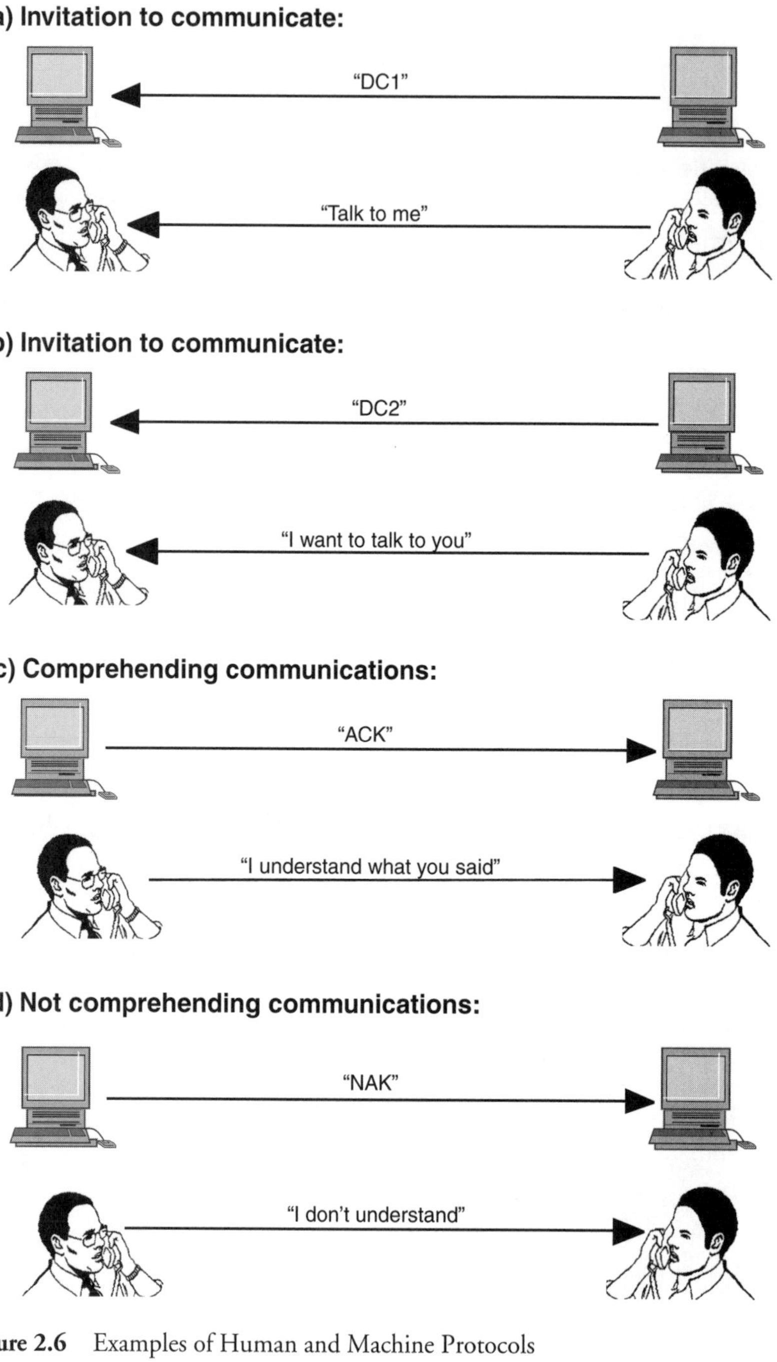

(a) Invitation to communicate:

"DC1"

"Talk to me"

(b) Invitation to communicate:

"DC2"

"I want to talk to you"

(c) Comprehending communications:

"ACK"

"I understand what you said"

(d) Not comprehending communications:

"NAK"

"I don't understand"

Figure 2.6   Examples of Human and Machine Protocols

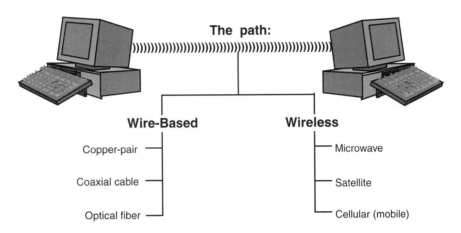

Figure 2.7   Examples of the Communications Link (the Media)

❏ Coaxial cable: This medium is the wire used for cable TV. It runs between our TV sets and the cable TV operator's office.

❏ Optical fiber: This medium uses light signals instead of electrical signals. The "wire" is made from glass (or plastic) rather than metal.

❏ Microwave: This medium uses the air as the transmission path and sends radio signals between stations.

❏ Satellite: This medium also uses the air as the transmission path, but one station is a satellite positioned above the earth to send and receive signals to and from a ground station.

❏ Cellular (mobile): This medium also uses the air for the path. Its distinguishing attribute is support of mobile stations, such as mobile phones.

In all these communications links, information in the form of 1s and 0s is transported between the computers. The 1s and 0s can be coded in different ways, depending on the medium technology. As noted earlier, some use voltages to represent the data, some use current flow, and some use light signals. The principal idea is that *everything* is represented as 1s and 0s. It is that simple.

Summary

It has been said that a rose by any other name is still a rose. Yes, and a SYN by any other name is still a SYN, unless it's spelled sin. Both SYN and sin are acts of computers and humans respectively, but we confine ourselves to the more prosaic SYN (and other computer actions) in this book.

We have learned that humans and computer networks are similar (to a limited extent) in that they both use languages and protocols to communicate. The computer's languages are called codes. The codes are formed by stringing together specific patterns of 1s and 0s.

Chapter 3

Sending and Receiving User Traffic on the Communications Link

In this chapter we look at two types of signals used in telephone and data networks. In so doing, we distinguish between voice and data signals. We also return to the subject of bits and learn how bits are sent across a communications link from one computer to a destination computer.

Another subject of this chapter is bandwidth. This term is defined and its importance is explained in the context of users and network service providers, such as telephone companies and Internet Service Providers (ISPs).

The chapter concludes by explaining how errors can occur during the transfer of data between computers, resulting in the destruction of the 1s and 0s in a message. We learn how these errors can distort the accuracy of the data transfer and influence the disposition and humor of the network customers who are affected by the errors.

Voice Signals

When Ted and Bob are talking over the telephone (or face-to-face), the speech is conveyed in analog signals, as shown in Figure 3.1. Analog signals transported across the telephone network are based on human speech. A person's speech produces various levels of air pressure that result in a sound wave being sent from the speaker's mouth to a listener's ears. When uttered into a telephone, the sound wave is translated into an electrical waveform representing the person's speech. Both sound waves and the telephone waveform have similar characteristics, but one is acoustical and the other is electrical.

Why is the voice signal on the telephone system called an analog signal? For one primary reason. The speech energy is a continuous signal in that it *gradually* changes its *amplitude*. The amplitude is the strength and electrical polarity

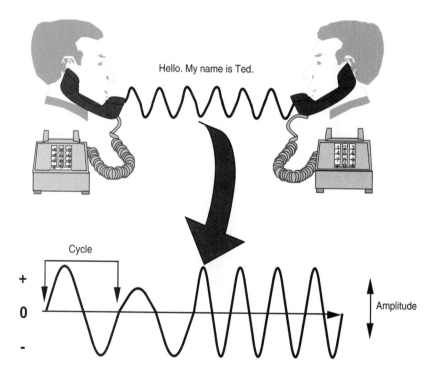

Figure 3.1 Audio/Voice Signals

of the signal, shown in Figure 3.1 as the height of the wave (its amplitude), and described in an electrical term, voltage.

Voltage is described in terms of a positive or negative electrical polarity. Thus, the speech signal gradually changes its voltage from zero to negative, back to zero, and then to positive, and finally back to zero, all measured in amplitude.

The signal repeats this process and goes through recurring cycles perhaps thousands or even millions of times per second. Thus, the term *cycles per second* describes how many of these transitions take place in one second.[1]

Voice and Data: There Is a Difference

Many data communications systems and computer-to-computer dialogues use the voice-oriented telephone local loop and the telephone local exchange (the LE or Central Office) for transmission and reception of data. Notwithstanding, data communications signals are quite different from voice communications signals. For example, voice signals are usually sent in a continuous stream (with the people talking most of the time), whereas data signals tend to be intermittent, or bursty (where the computers don't "talk" all the time). As we piece together the Networking 101 puzzle, we will have more to say about voice and data networks and why computers are intermittent communicators.

Data and Voice: The Historical Dependency

For this discussion, we should note that the data communications technology and industry are relatively new and began their rapid ascent into our lives during the 1960s. Telephone networks preceded data networks by many decades.

In hindsight, if the appropriate technology had been available when data communications systems evolved in the mid-1900s, the voice-oriented telephone network would not have been used for data communications between computers. However, the telephone network was "there." It provided a readily

---

1. The term cycles per second is not used much anymore. The more common term is hertz. The term hertz honors a noted engineer named Hertz who contributed to communications theory.

available worldwide transmission medium for the data communications systems to use.

It is a moot point now, so let's examine the data signals. Later, we will learn how the data signals between computers are transported by the telephone network.

Data Signals

In contrast to analog signals, which convey the fluctuations in voice transmissions, computer signals are composed of digital images that represent the discrete signal states of 1 and 0, as introduced in Chapter 2. Since computer signals use binary schemes (for example, in transistors) where the bits are coded as 1 or 0, digital signaling is an ideal scheme for the transmission of computer traffic.

As one example, in a simple digital system, a 0 can be represented by a positive voltage of at least +3 volts and a 1 can be represented by a negative voltage of at least -3 volts. The idea is shown in Figure 3.2.

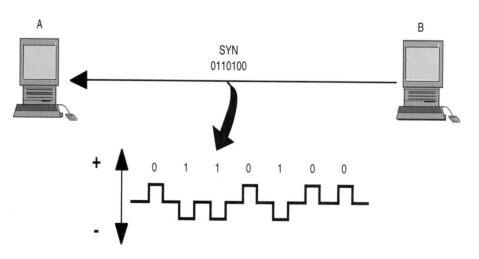

Figure 3.2 Data Signals

This uncomplicated scheme is sufficient to provide the digital signals to create codes, such as the code for SYN (explained in Chapter 2) by simply altering the voltage level within a computer or on a transmission link. It is no more complicated than understanding that the AA batteries in our appliances produce or do not produce voltages.

Because the signal is changed abruptly by voltage shifts, a discrete signal is produced. This situation is exactly what data transmissions require—a discrete signal to represent either 1s or 0s.

Is the Link Analog or Digital?

One concept to keep in mind. The link itself (the medium), such as the telephone wires in a home, is the same for analog or digital signals. What is different is the sending and receiving equipment on each end of this link. For an analog line, the equipment is the telephone, and for a digital line, the equipment is a computer.

This link is the same for both types of transmissions. If digital signals are sent from a computer out of a home to the Internet, those signals are going over the same wire as the telephone analog voice conversations. What makes a digital link is *not* the link itself, but the transmitter and receiver that are attached to the link.

As another example, think of the air as a medium for our analog voice transmissions. It is also the medium for digital signals, for example, the conveyance of on/off flashes of a flashlight. The medium remains the same; the "equipment" differs.

Additional information is provided on using the computer digital signal on the telephone analog link in later chapters.

Bits and Codes on the Link

The next part of the analysis explains in more detail how computer communications links function and describes some problems that can occur in these systems. Upon the first encounter with these ideas, some of them seem a bit complicated. But upon reflection, we realize that they are elegantly simple.

We could ignore these subjects and go on to the next chapter. But if we did, we would miss the opportunity to understand one of the most important concepts in computer networks: *bandwidth*.

An Example of Bits and Codes

Figure 3.3 is an example of a digital transmission. Chapter 2 explained the NAK code, which means negative acknowledgment, a computer's method of stating that a transmission it received from another computer was not understood. It usually means the message was garbled during the transmission, and the receiving computer can't make out what the message means. For example, the error could have occurred because of static on the link.

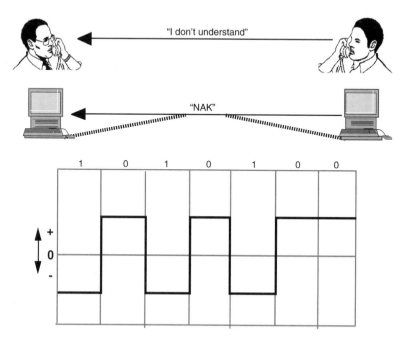

Figure 3.3 Bits and Codes on the Link

Notice that the NAK code is the binary string of 1010100.[2] These images are conveyed across a communications link, such as the wires on your telephone line, with electrical signals. In this example, these electrical signals are used: a 0 is represented by a positive voltage, and a 1 by a negative voltage.

Don't forget: the information could also be represented by the absence or presence of electrical energy. For example, if the sending machine's transmitter were turned off for a brief time, this time on the link could represent a 1; if the machine's transmitter were turned on for a brief time, this time could represent a 0.

Another Example of Bits and Codes

Another approach to represent 1s and 0s is used in optical systems, which send light signals. In this situation, the sender can represent a 1 as a flash of light, and a 0 by turning the light transmitter off—something like we did as children by sending codes with a flashlight, or the old navies did when using light semaphore between ships. The receiving machine is designed to recognize the presence or absence of light signals as a string of 1s or 0s, respectively, and then assemble these binary strings to form the codes. Figure 3.4 uses a light bulb to depict the idea.

A light bulb is appropriate for our general examples, but computer networks that use optical signals employ special light signals that are not intended for the human eye. The sending and receiving machines have special senders and receivers for these transmissions. It is likely you have read about them; they are called optical fiber systems and were introduced in Chapter 2. Whatever optical form the signals take, they are still sending and receiving 1s and 0s that constitute codes, such as the NAK in this example.

Figure 3.4 introduces another important concept. At the bottom of the figure is a depiction of the time (the duration) the bits are represented on the

---

2. In modern computer networks, it has become common practice to use a more efficient way of representing a NAK (and an ACK). Instead of a full 7-bit byte, a very small nibble of one bit is used. The "ACK/NAK" nibble is placed in a specific place in the message, such that the receiving computer always knows which position at which this nibble bit is located. Then, this one-bit nibble value of 1 can represent a NAK, and the counterpart of 0 can represent an ACK.

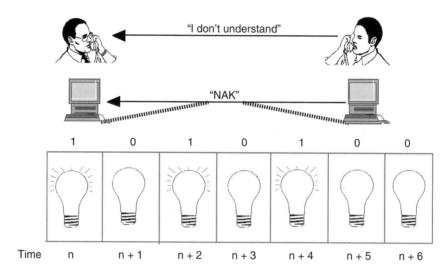

Figure 3.4   Using Other Modes of Signal Representation

communications link, that is, how long the transmitter sends a flash of light, and how long the transmitter is turned off and nothing is sent.

At time *n* a 1 is represented: at time *n* + 1, a 0 is represented, and so on. Therefore, the sending machine is sending periodic light flashes or nothing at all. These images represent periodic signals of 1s and 0s at the receiving machine.

Bit Cell and Time

Each bit is called a *bit cell*. The bit cell represents how long the bit remains on the communications link, that is, how long the sending machine sends each bit. For example, the sending computer may represent a bit cell by sending a 1 or 0 on the link for a very brief time. Let's say it sets the link to a positive voltage for .001 seconds (one millisecond), and uses the same amount of time to represent a negative voltage. Figure 3.5 illustrates the example.

There are 1,000 milliseconds in a second (1 second divided by .001 = 1,000). If these machines are sending and receiving 1,000 bit cells every sec-

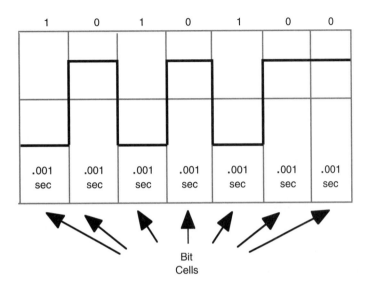

Figure 3.5 Bit Cells and Bit Times

ond, they are said to be operating at 1,000 bits per second (or 1 kbit/s, where k stands for kilo, or one thousand).

Bits, Bandwidth, and Broadband Networks

Communications networks are measured by their capacity, stated in how many bits per second they send and receive.[3] This capacity is called *bandwidth*. There are other definitions of bandwidth, but this one is appropriate for this discussion. The system in Figure 3.5 has a bandwidth capacity of 1 kbit/s.

---

3. Why can't the bandwidth of a network be measured in bits per minute, or bits per hour, or even bits per year? One reason is that modern networks can transmit millions or even billions of bits per second over a link from one machine to another. If bandwidth were measured in (for example) bits per minute, the numbers would become so large they would be hard to read or write.

A system with a large capacity, a high bandwidth, is also called a high-speed system. In this context, speed refers to bits per second, not how fast the bits are traveling on the communications link. All images, digital or analog, propagate across the communications link at about the same speed (the speed of light). How many of the bits that are propagated in one second determines the bandwidth of the system.

Some high-capacity networks today are no longer called high-speed networks. The term is still used, and that is why it is explained here. Another common term for high-capacity networks is *broadband* networks.

Broadband People

I recently heard a person refer to someone's intelligence in relation to bandwidth. The person was described as "She has a lot of bandwidth." Bill Gates has been described as a person with a broadband mind.

I don't deny Mr. Gates' intelligence or that of the woman, but the term bandwidth is misused for this description.

Processing a lot of bits in a specific time (one second in computer networks) is the current definition of the term broadband. But processing a lot of bits (information) does not necessarily mean the processing is of high quality. As Thoreau said in *Walden,* "After all, the man whose horse trots a mile in a minute does not [necessarily] carry the most important message."

Still, I think I might be offended if someone called me a low bandwidth person. But this term might be preferable to a term I heard recently in another conversation, virtual bandwidth: a person who thinks he or she possesses intelligence but does not. My thoughts on these buzzwords is that they are harmless to our language, and add some fun to our discourses with each other.

The Importance of Bandwidth

Recall that the example system has a bandwidth of 1,000 bits per second. If a NAK signal requires seven bits to be represented, then the sending of the NAK consumes $7/1000^{th}$ of the capacity of the link for the one-second period.

This simple idea has profound implications for computer networks for it deals with the capacity of networks to transport information between computers.

To illustrate, Ted's email to Bob contains a message of several paragraphs of sentences consisting of words and letters (characters). For this example, the email is 700 characters (As, Bs, Cs, etc.).[4]

Again, each letter is represented by seven bits. Therefore, 700 characters × 7 bits per character = 4,900 bits. If the communications system is sending the email at 1,000 bit/s, it will take 4.9 seconds (4,900 / 1000 = 4.9) to send this very short email message!

If Ted were to send Bob a large file consisting of millions of characters, which is quite common, it might take several hours to send all this information on a 1 kbit/s communications link. Fortunately, this is just an example, and the computers and other equipment we use today have considerably more bandwidth than 1 kbit/s.

Low Bandwidth Equals Unhappy Users

Nonetheless, a low-bandwidth system presents immense problems to effective communications. You know this sad fact if you have logged on to the Internet and tried to get information from, say, a news service, a stock report, even a photograph. Sometimes it takes several seconds, and sometimes it takes several minutes. Why? Because of the lack of bandwidth.[5]

Therefore, it is of paramount importance that communications networks be able to send and receive information at a high bit rate, that is, to exhibit broadband characteristics. The higher the bit rate, the more bandwidth, and the more information the network can transport in a given time.

Additionally, you can now see why it is advantageous for you to have a "high-speed" connection to the Internet: you get more capacity and are given faster response time. And you are a happier user of the network.

---

4. In all these calculations, we are making some assumptions, such as: Ted and Bob have exclusive use of the link and there are no other bits on the link. Later discussions refine these examples.
5. The delay may also be attributable to the Internet's computers, such as Web servers, that could be too busy to provide fast service.

One Way to Increase Bandwidth

One approach to increasing the bit-carrying capacity of the network is to shorten the length (time duration) of the bit cell; that is, decrease the time the bit is represented on the communications link.[6] To illustrate this idea, the well-known DS1 technology developed by the Bell System in the 1960s operates at 1,544,000 bit/s (1.544 Mbit/s, for megabits per second). Its bit cell is 648 nanoseconds (ns): 1/1,544,000 = .000000648 seconds.

With this technology, the NAK code now consumes only 7/1,544,000[th] of the capacity of this high-speed link, which leaves capacity for other transmissions. Furthermore, our 700-character email would take only .00317 seconds to transmit (700 characters × 7 bits per character × .000000648 seconds per character = .00317).

So, once again, one of most important aspects of computer networks is their information-carrying capacity, stated in bit/s, and described by the term bandwidth.

Why We Don't Have this Bandwidth at Our Computers?

It appears that this large capacity is not available in many networks, especially those that connect to our personal computers at home. After all, it may take several seconds or even minutes to download information from the Internet to a PC.

This appearance is valid. The telephone wires (local loop) connecting most residences to networks are of very low capacity. The links inside the network that connect the switches are broadband links, so the traffic moves at high speed in parts of the end-to-end connection between Ted and Bob, but not on the final leg (the final mile) between these users. This idea is explained in more detail in Chapter 6.

---

6. Other factors come into play that are beyond our discussion, for example, compression and multilevel coding, subjects slated for Networking 102.

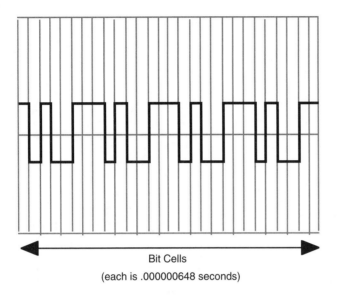

Bit Cells
(each is .000000648 seconds)

Figure 3.6 Making the Bits Shorter in Time

To reiterate: At the risk of overemphasis, look at these relationships (and please refer to Figure 3.10 at the end of this chapter for more details):

- ❒ Decreasing the bit length means
- ❒ increasing the bit rate, which translates to
- ❒ increasing network capacity, which is the same as
- ❒ increasing bandwidth, leading to
- ❒ happy users.

Why Not Make the Bit Lengths Even Shorter in Time?

You may be thinking at this point: Why not just continue to shorten the length of the bit cell, since its length is inversely proportional to the bit rate, as depicted in Figure 3.6? The shorter the bit is, the more bits the link can carry, which results in more bits per second, that is, more bandwidth.

This idea can be implemented to a point. But beyond that point, the bit becomes so short (in time) that it cannot be interpreted correctly. It becomes

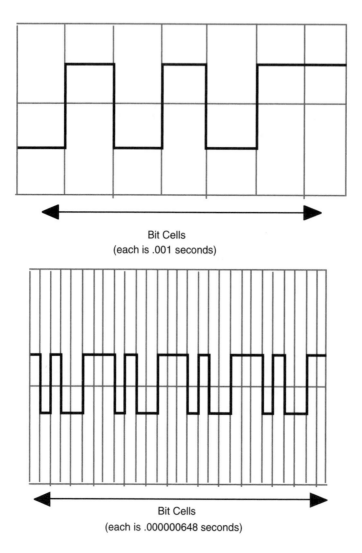

Figure 3.7 Comparison of Two Bandwidths

so tiny that it cannot be detected, or it is subject to distortion due to, say, static (noise) on the link. In so many words, a short bit cell is not "robust." This chapter explains more about robustness shortly.

Before leaving this subject, recall that bandwidth refers to the capacity of a link or network to carry traffic, stated in bit/s. In our simple example, the

1,000 bit/s link is a low bandwidth link and the DS1 1.544 Mbit/s link is a high bandwidth link (a broadband link). Of course, it is now easy to understand the statement: the more bandwidth the better.

Comparison of Two Different Bandwidths

To reinforce the idea of bandwidth in relation to bit time, let's compare the two earlier illustrations (see Figure 3.7). Notice that the very small bit cell times allow more bits to be placed on the communications link in the 1-second period. The figure is not proportional, since the very small bit cell of = .000000648 seconds cannot be drawn in relation to the longer bit cell of .001 seconds. Nonetheless, it is easy to see the relationship of bandwidth to bit cell duration.

Why Longer Bits Are More Robust

Let's return to the subject of robustness. The 1 or 0 bit can remain on the link for a longer time; it can have a long duration. That, in turn, makes it more robust. For example, if static (called noise) is on the link, the longer bit cell is more impervious to this static than is a short-bit cell. In effect, the longer bit cell is more easily detected at the receiver in the presence of problems, such as static.

Here are some other examples. First, consider Morse code. Telegraph operators sometimes had trouble comprehending the received signals if the sending operator keyed them in too fast: the signals were on the line for too brief a time and were difficult to detect. Second, consider the light semaphore that Navy ships use (more for show today). If a sending operator flashes the signals too quickly, the receiving operator has trouble receiving them; the light signal's "bit cells" are too short.

And yet another example. I am from New Mexico. When I moved to the East, I had trouble understanding some conversations with people from New York, because they spoke too fast. And yet, some of my friends from Georgia had the same problem with the "bit rate" of my conversation: it was too fast for correct detection.

Bit Decay: Like Running Through Water

Another point should be made at this stage in the analysis. It deals with decay or attenuation. The strength of a signal decays (attenuates) as it travels through a transmission path. The amount of attenuation depends on a number of factors that are beyond this general discussion. But think of attenuation like the case of a man trying to run through a pool of water five feet deep. After a while, his energy dissipates because of the resistance of the water, and he slows down. Sending the 1s and 0s through a wire or through the air is the same idea. The wire and the air also offer resistance, leading to the decay of the strength of the signal.

The cogent aspect of this situation is that a combination of noise and attenuation and other impairments could distort the bit such that it might be misinterpreted at the receiving machine.

In Figure 3.8, the sending computer is sending out the character J to the receiving computer. However, it does not arrive as a J. Because of noise and signal decay, the J is interpreted as a special code LF, which means line feed. Notice that the seventh bit has been distorted. It was coded as a 1 at the sender but received as a 0 at the receiver.

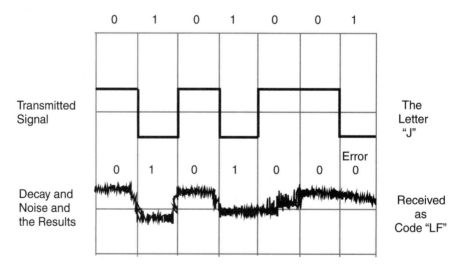

Figure 3.8   A Data Error

One bit "destroyed"

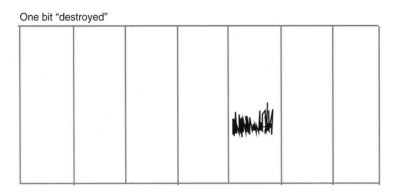

Multiple bits "destroyed"

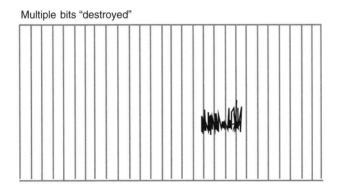

Figure 3.9   Comparison of Two Errors

The LF code is usually used to control a line feed (the carriage return) on a printer—not exactly what the sending machine intended for the receiving machine to do. In fact, if these bits are in the email messages, they have no meaning. If they are in a different message (e.g., a control message destined for a printer), they would be used to instruct the printer to do a carriage return. In this example, link impairments caused an error.

Now we can visualize the idea of robustness. In Figure 3.9, the communications link experiences some noise from factors such as lightning in the air, interference from someone's radio, etc. Even a household appliance can create noise on a link.

For the long-bit cell, only one bit is destroyed. But for the system that uses short-bit cells, multiple bits are damaged.[7] The result of this situation is that high-speed networks (broadband networks) must deal with the probability that a link passing by, say, an electrical power plant will be subject to a lot of interference, resulting in possible damage to the 1 or 0 bits and errors in the transmission. The same problem exists in mobile phones when the phone user passes a high-power line.

Are Errors a Problem?

Are these errors a problem? It depends on the nature of the user traffic. Some transmissions can afford to have bits damaged, and others cannot. Let's imagine your funds transfer to your Swiss bank account has an error that results in the "shifting" of a decimal point in the data. Once again, is this error a problem? Obviously, it depends on which direction the decimal point was shifted; it may be no problem at all to you, but it might be a problem for the bank manager. The old adage, "Where one stands on an issue depends on where one sits," is apropos for this example.

Errors are a big problem if they are handled improperly. Several years ago, I showed up at the wrong airport because one of my friends and I were using our own communications software to send messages to each other. One of our dialogues dealt with our travel plans. We had not yet taken the time to write some error-detection software, which would have checked to determine if the bits in the messages were being sent correctly. The end result was that my friend sent me a message declaring that he would meet me at "SFO" at a given time and place. The message was damaged and I received it as "SJO." I sent back to him a message confirming our meeting. He went to the San Francisco airport and I went to the San Jose airport: an event today known as a virtual meeting.

---

7. Many ways to combat transmission impairments do not deal with maintaining a long-bit cell. Indeed, during the past three decades, techniques have been developed to allow very short bit durations, very high bit rates, and very low error rates. We use the bit cell duration idea to make some points about bandwidth and robustness. And the idea is valid, but it does simplify what is a very complex subject. Well, that's Networking 101, but a general explanation of these more advanced ideas is provided in the last section of this chapter.

No Bits Shall Be in Error!

Generally, most computer networks assume that no bits can be in error, and they take extensive measures to guarantee the safe delivery of every single bit sent between Ted and Bob—an impressive service that we will examine in later parts of this book.

Error Detection: Computers and Humans

A pause here might be helpful. A computer is not very intelligent. If a bit is distorted and results in a changed message, the computer may display it on a screen (unless it asks for a retransmission). It is quite rare to see a screen displayed with errors (misspelled words, erroneous graphics). The reason is that most networks execute these retransmissions until all the bits are received without errors, usually within fractions of a second.

In contrast, we humans possess remarkable inferential skills. If we receive a voice "transmission" that is in error (say, garbled), we usually know something is amiss. In many instances, we can infer the correct meaning to the missing or distorted information. Otherwise, we ask for clarification, that is, a retransmission. Computers are not very intuitive, and they must be programmed to detect errors and ask for a retransmission, with the NAK signal.

Multilevel Coding

Before leaving the subject of bit rates and bandwidth, we should note that more elaborate systems are available that have a way of representing more than 1 or 0 within a bit cell. This idea may seem impossible, but it is a rather easy task, and Samuel Morse came up with the idea when he was working on the telegraph over 150 years ago. Figure 3.10 shows how.

The technology uses a method called *multilevel coding*. On the left side of the figure, two possible signals are coded (and interpreted) as 0 or 1. Therefore, the signal is allowed to take on only two states, for example, two different voltage levels. Therefore, each bit cell contains one bit.

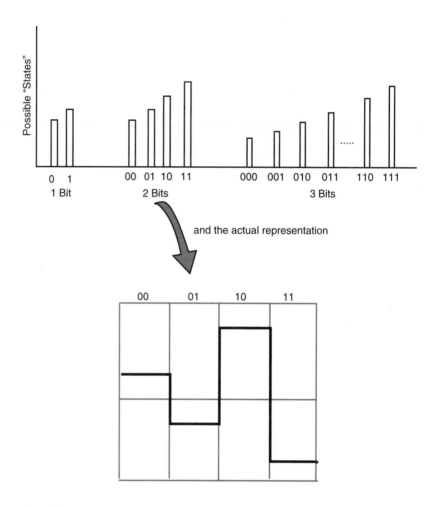

Result: One-bit cell carries two bits, and the capacity of the link is doubled.

Figure 3.10   Multilevel Coding

In the middle of the figure, the signal can take on any one of four possible states. Consequently, a single bit cell can be coded to represent any combination of two bits (00, 01, 10, or 11). In this scheme, each bit cell contains two bits.

On the right side of the figure, eight possible states can represent any one of eight 3-bit codes, ranging from 000 to 111. In this scheme, each bit cell contains three bits.

This multilevel coding can be expanded to have one bit cell represent hundreds of states, which translates to *hundreds of bits per bit cell.*

This technique is so common that it is almost universal in the communications products we use every day. When you dial in to your bank teller, the stock broker, or just about anyone, your machine is performing multilevel coding in order to give you more bandwidth. That is why you may see on your computer screen notations like "28,800 bits per second," "57,000 bits per second," and so on. Based on the quality of the link between the computers, special devices called *modems* are adjusting their behavior to give you the "best" performance possible. The next chapter explains the modem and how it provides this service.

Summary

Broadband networks, broadband people—both process a lot of information in a given time. The quality of the information processing is another matter. But to place the terms in their proper context: A broadband network is one in which many bits per second are transported. A broadband person is one in whom many "bits per second" are absorbed, comprehended, and perhaps relayed to someone else.

I do a small injustice to broadband networks in this restricted definition, in that they are capable of making some rather "intelligent" decisions. We will learn about these intelligent capabilities in subsequent chapters.

In this chapter, we learned that computer networks have a simple way of representing information: the use of electrical or optical signals to convey 1s and 0s between computers. And the more 1s and 0s that can be sent between these machines, the faster customers and users can send and receive traffic, such as email, stock quotes, photographs, and so on.

We now know that these ideas relate to the concept of bandwidth. In relation to a low bandwidth network, a high bandwidth network transports more bits per second between network customers, resulting in faster response time, higher throughput, and more-satisfied customers.

Chapter 4

The Modem and the Telephone Network

This chapter introduces the modem, a key piece of the Networking 101 puzzle. It explains how the modem sends data over a telephone network. We examine how the modem places 1s and 0s onto the telephone wire at the sending site and removes them at the receiving site. The chapter also examines how the modem is connected to computers and to the telephone plug in homes and offices.

Defining the Problem

The previous chapters discussed analog telephone traffic and digital computer traffic. Remember that the telephone system is designed for analog signals, as shown in Figure 4.1(a). How can discrete digital bits of 1s and 0s be sent over the telephone network, which was designed for the transmission of nondiscrete analog voice signals?

From the technical perspective, it is certainly possible to redesign the analog system so that it will carry the digital signals, but such a redesign would be an expensive process. Can you imagine how great the task would be of replacing all the analog telephones (and other components in the telephone offices) with digital telephone systems? It would cost billions of dollars.

The answer is obvious. There must be a method of using the current system (the telephone), yet provide a means to send data over it.

Examining the Solution

To use the analog telephone signal for data transmission (digital transmission), the data communications industry developed a relatively simple device called a *modem*. The term is a derivative of the words *mod*ulator and *dem*odulator. Figure 4.1(b) shows the placement of the modem in relation to the computer and the communications link.

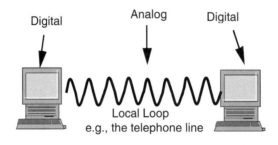

(a) The Analog Link

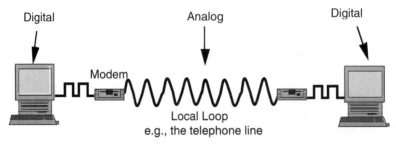

(b) The Digital and Analog Signals

Figure 4.1 The Problem? Interfacing the Telephone and Computer Worlds

This machine is taken for granted today. It is a commonplace appliance. But its impact on our professional and personal lives has been profound. Without the modem, it would have been impossible to build computer networks on a large scale. These networks would have been relegated to support a very small part of the population—those who had native-mode digital interfaces from the user machines to the network. That population was and is very small. Indeed, the Internet would not be the presence it is today if the modem had not been invented.

A Small Point About the Example

Figure 4.1(b) shows the modem as an external device to the user computer. The arrangement at your PC may not look like this example. As an alternative, the modem is often installed inside the cover of the PC. It may also be a line card that plugs into a slot on the PC. Later examples show these configurations.

Modulation Methods

Several basic modulation methods are employed by modems. Some modems use more than one of the methods. Each method impresses the data signal on an analog *carrier* signal, which is altered to carry the 1s and 0s of the digital data stream; thus the term carrier. This modulated carrier is sent by the transmitting modem across the communications link. At the receiver modem, the 1s and 0s are removed (demodulated) from the carrier, and presented to the computer. Figure 4.2 illustrates how modulation works.

The modulation methods are called amplitude modulation, frequency modulation and phase modulation. Amplitude modulation is described here in a general way. In keeping with Networking 101, the description does not delve into the details of these modulation techniques. Indeed, trying to explain phase modulation is pushing the subject into Networking 102, or even 103.

But the subject is quite important, so the focus of the discussion is on the first method. The other two methods are explained in Appendix B.

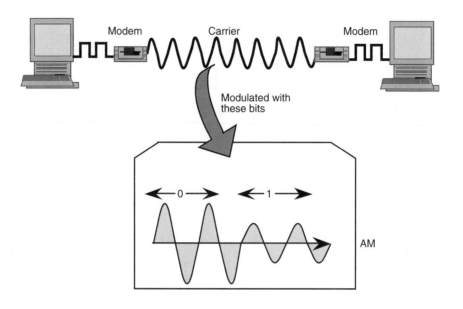

Figure 4.2 The Solution … Modulation

Amplitude modulation alters the amplitude of the analog signal in accordance with the 1s and 0s of the digital bit stream. It is similar to the digital techniques described earlier, except that the 1s and 0s are represented by high and low amplitudes of the analog signal, and not digital pulses.

Connecting to the Telephone Network

Most connections between user machines, such as PCs, take place through the telephone system. As Figure 4.3 shows, the PC's modem is connected to a telephone wall jack in a house. This connection is extended through the telephone company's (Telco's) wires (the local loop) to a nearby telephone Central Office. This extension is achieved by connecting the wire in the house to the wire that goes to the Central Office. It is usually done at a junction box that the telephone company attaches to the outside of the house.

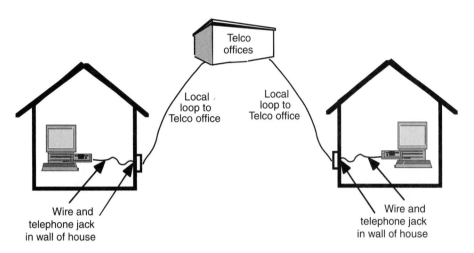

Figure 4.3　Connecting to the Telephone System

The PC and the modem are usually programmed to automatically dial up the called party, just as a person does when manually dialing a number on a telephone. After the dial-up operations are completed, the modem then accepts the outgoing 1s and 0s from the computer, and modulates the outgoing analog signal to "carry" these bits to the telephone Central Office. At this office they are then relayed across the network to the destination user, the called party.

Sending Ted's "Payload" to Bob

The chat message, a file, a spreadsheet, and so forth from Ted to Bob is called payload. As noted earlier, it is so named because it should produce income for the service providers who are transporting Ted's message to Bob. Examples of service providers are telephone companies, such as AT&T, and Internet Service Providers (ISPs), such as AOL and MSN. They charge the user a fee for using their networks, so the user's traffic is "payload" to them.

In Figure 4.4, the payload from Ted to Bob is being transported through the telephone network. The bold lines in the figure indicate the path the payload takes from Ted's computer to Bob's computer.

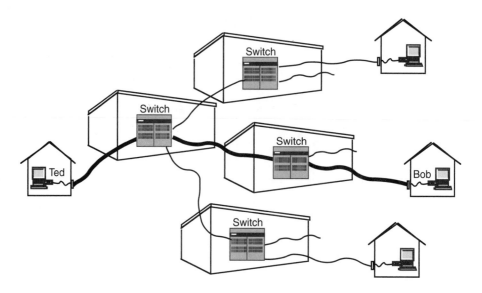

Figure 4.4   The Path Through the Telephone Network

The Interface

The term *interface* describes the point at a computer (or some other machine such as printer) in which the wire is connected to the machine. At the back of a computer are printer cables (really bundles of wires), mouse cables, and so forth connected to the machine. There may also be a telephone line connected to it. These connections are also called interfaces.

The Switch

The payload is sent to Ted's local Central Office where it passes though several components (some of them are not shown here). The one of prime interest is a switch, introduced in Chapter 1. As its name implies, the job of the switch is to switch (relay) traffic (the payload) from the incoming link at the switch onto an outgoing link. This introductory example shows a telephone switch, called a circuit switch. Later, other switches are introduced.

The switch is programmed to know the best outgoing link interface to eventually reach Bob. Later, we will see how the switch can be so smart. For now, we can say that the payload, initially sent by Ted, can be sent end-to-end to arrive at Bob's machine. And when it does arrive, Bob's machine announces to him, "You've got mail," or some other form of an alert.

Don't forget that other machines may be involved in this process, such as a mail server. They are not shown here. Take a look at Appendix A to learn more about these machines.

Location of the Modem

I noted that in many computers the modem is not a separate unit but is housed within the cover of the computer. This modem is called an in-board modem. The access to the modem is through a connector on the side or on the back of the machine, as shown in Figure 4.5. Recall that this connector is called an interface.

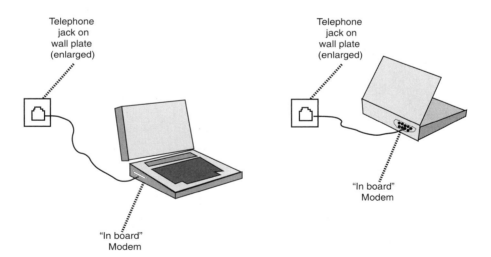

Figure 4.5   The Modem Interface

The modem interface varies, depending on the choice made by the computer manufacturer. It may be a proprietary plug, it might be a conventional telephone jack, or it might be a connector that is standardized by a trade group, such as the Electronics Industries Association.

The connector to the telephone wire in a building or home is a conventional telephone jack, which plugs into the a wall socket, also shown in Figure 4.5.

Summary

Alas, the poor modem does not get the accolades it deserves. It is such a common instrument that we take it for granted, much like we treat telephones. But the modem has had a profound impact on our lives. It is likely you would not be using the Internet (and it is likely I would not be writing this book) if it were not for the modem.

In this chapter, we learned about the purpose of the modem, how it sends data over a telephone network. We showed how the modem places 1s and 0s onto the telephone wire at the sending site and removes them at the receiving site. We also examined the modem's interface, with examples of how it is connected to the computer and the telephone wall jack.

Chapter 5

▷ # Digital Networks

This chapter continues the discussions on analog and digital systems, with the emphasis on digital networks. The advantages of digital networks are described, with examples of how the telephone system sends voice conversations in digital form. The operations to translate analog voice signals into digital images are also explained.

Advantages of Digital Networks

All-digital networks were developed to overcome some of the limitations of analog systems. Several problems arise regarding the analog voice signal and how it is transmitted across the communications link, as shown in Figure 5.1.

First, the analog signal is relayed through the telephone system through components called *amplifiers*. These devices are designed to boost the strength of the signal as it makes its way through the network. Recall that the signal decays (attenuates) as it is sent through a wire, somewhat like a person who gets tired from a long walk or a run.

The amplifier boosts the strength of the signal. A person may also get a boost during a walk or run. This boost may entail taking a rest or drinking some liquid. But Ted's email's signals (the 1s and 0s) are not allowed to take a rest. They must be sent through the network without delay, something like marathon runners grabbing a cup of water from a refreshment stand as they run by the stand.

The amplifiers must perform the boosting function such that the analog waveform representing the signal maintains its characteristics from one end of the network to the other. A deviation from this consistency creates a distortion of the waveform and could result in Bob's modem misinterpreting Ted's incoming payload.

In addition, there is the problem of static (noise) on the link. As the signal travels through the network, the noise mixes with the signal, sometimes to the point where all one can hear on the line is static. Of course, this extreme situation is rare, but noise is always present and it distorts the signal.

All analog signals exhibit some form of distortion. Unfortunately, the intervening components to strengthen the signal, such as amplifiers, distort the signal by also amplifying the noise.

Digital systems overcome these problems by representing the transmitted data with digital, binary images. The analog signal is converted to a series of digital 1s and 0s and transmitted through the communications channel as binary data. So, the analog signal is not used; it is replaced by a digital signal.

Take a look at the final signals in Figure 5.1. In Figure 5.1(a), the reconstituted (resultant) analog signal is distorted and "fuzzy." In Figure 5.1(b), the resultant digital signal is quite sharp and "clean."

Digital signals are subject to the same kinds of imperfections and problems as the analog signal: decay of the strength of the signal and the noise that is interjected into the link. However, recall that the digital signal is discrete: the binary representations of the analog waveform are represented by varying levels of voltages, in contrast to the nondiscrete levels of an analog signal. Indeed, an analog signal has almost infinite variability.

As the digital signal traverses the link, it is only necessary to sample the absence or presence of a digital binary pulse–not its degree, as in the analog signal.

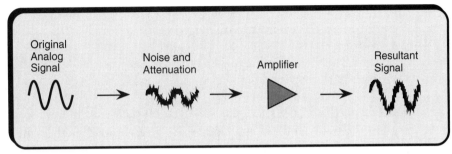

(a) Analog Reconstruction

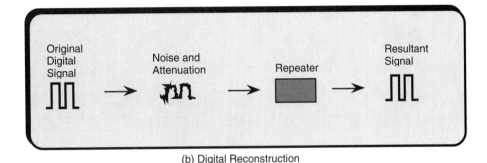

(b) Digital Reconstruction

Figure 5.1　Digital vs. Analog Systems

The mere absence or presence of a signal pulse can be more easily recognized than can the amplitude or phase of an analog signal. If the digital signal is examined (sampled) at an acceptable rate (many times per bit cell) and at an acceptable voltage level, the 1 or 0 can then be completely reconstituted before it deteriorates below a minimum threshold. This operation is not performed by an amplifier, but by a regenerative repeater, usually called a *repeater*.

Since noise and attenuation can be completely eliminated from the reconstructed signal, the digital signal can tolerate the problems of noise and attenuation much better than can the analog signal.

These attributes of digital systems are why most of our telephone conversations today are so clear. (Cell phones are excluded from this example.) If you recall the predigital days, it was not unusual to have telephone conversations in which there was as much static (noise) on the line, especially a long distance connection, as there was the voice signal.

Digital Voice

Thus far in this book, the focus has been on data transmissions, with secondary emphasis on voice. Data signals are already in digital form, so they are conveyed through an all-digital network without a lot of translations. The same cannot be said for Ted's and Bob's voice transmissions. Since they are analog, they must be translated into digital 1s and 0s if they are to be transported across digital links.

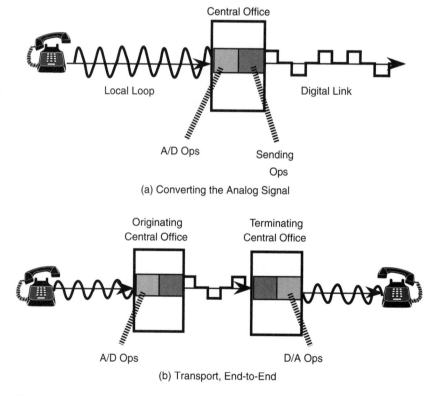

(a) Converting the Analog Signal

(b) Transport, End-to-End

Figure 5.2   Digital Voice Transmissions: Basic Concepts

In a typical digital telephone system, the customer's analog voice signals are converted to digital signals at the telephone Central Office. Figure 5.2 (a) provides a general view of the process. The local loop terminates the user telephone signal at the Central Office. Conventional analog signals are sent to the Central Office, where an analog-to-digital conversion (A/D) takes place. The digital signals are then placed onto another link (an outgoing interface) and sent through the network to another user.

In Figure 5.2 (b), the incoming digital traffic to the receiving user is taken through a reverse process at the Central Office. The traffic is converted back to analog (the D/A) operation and sent to the receiving user's telephone.

Analog-to-Digital Conversion

Several methods are employed to change an analog voice signal into a representative string of digital binary images. Even though these methods entail many processes, the idea is to examine the voice signal and convert it to 1s and 0s. This examination is called *sampling*.

The idea behind sampling is to examine the voice signal often, well, very often. The accepted sampling rate in the industry is 8,000 samples per second. This high sampling rate allows the accurate reproduction of the analog waveform of the sampled speech signal.

This operation is shown in Figure 5.3. With 8,000 samples per second, the essential characteristics of a voice signal are captured. As the figure shows, the samples actually model the waveform of the audio speech. Now it may be easier to understand why so many samples are needed. If just a few samples per second were employed, the characteristics of the voice signal would not be accurately reflected in the samples.

You have probably heard a digital voice image that sounded "tinny" and phony. Some automated answering machines sound very poor. Part of the reason is that the sampled voice was not sampled enough times to reflect the person's speech traits. Another example is the mobile phone. Some mobile phone (cellular) systems are not very good in relation to quality. Some do

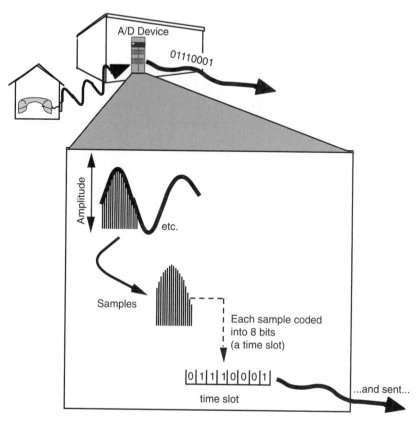

Figure 5.3 Voice: Analog-to-Digital (A/D) Conversion

not sound "accurate," and one reason may be that the caller's voice is not sampled enough.

With some license taken with the Jerry Lee Lewis song, he could not have said it better: "A whole lot of sampling going on" is the keystone of high-quality digital voice traffic.[1]

---

1. Other factors affect the quality of digital voice, but they are not important for these introductory discussions. See the references in Chapter 20 if you want to know more about digital voice technology.

By the way, if each sample of the speech is converted to 8 bits, and the speech is sampled at a rate of 8,000 times per second, the bandwidth requirement for the digital telephone conversation is 64,000 bits per second (8 bits × 8,000 = 64,000). You may have heard of or read about the 64 bit/s rate. Now you know the reason for its existence.[2]

It's All a Matter of 1s and 0s

Something quite extraordinary has been described during these last discussions. Take another look at Figure 5.3. The voice samples have been converted to 1s and 0s. In effect, each sample is assigned a digital code of 8 bits. Why is this operation extraordinary? Because it allows a network to transport voice and data in the same format—1s and 0s—which in turn provides the opportunity of using just one network for both voice and data.

The All-Digital Network

It is only a matter of time before the separate voice and data networks of the world merge together. This merger has been underway since the advent of digital voice over four decades ago. I often use the Internet, a data network, for my voice conversations with my business colleagues. Sometimes the voice quality leaves something to be desired, but it gets the job done. For an example of this process, see scenario 7 in Appendix A.

An all-digital network supports the operations shown in Figure 5.4, in which the computer hello of SYN is sent in digital form and so is Ted's hello to Bob. Everything is digital inside the network.

In the near future, everything in the network and on the local loop will be represented as 1s and 0s, including video, fax, voice, photographs, spreadsheets, slide shows, and of course, data. As noted, almost all forms of human and computer communications are already sent in digital form.

---

2. The bit rate of 64 kbit/s is the prevalent method used in conventional telephone networks. Other systems, such as mobile phone networks, and the Internet use more effective digital voice schemes. These systems can represent a high-quality voice signal with far fewer bits, ranging from 5–13 kbit/s.

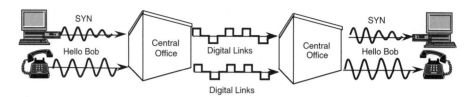

Figure 5.4   The All-Digital Network

When you speak on the telephone to someone, it is very likely that your speech is converted at the telephone office into the digital codes we have discussed in this chapter.

Perhaps you can now see why we have spent so much time in this book showing the transmission of 1s and 0s.

Summary

We often hear about the virtues of digital networks. Many TV advertisements tout their worthy distinctions. One commercial shows the clarity with which the sound of a pin dropping onto a table can be detected in a digital network. We now know what digital networks are: all traffic is encoded into digital 1s and 0s.

An all-digital network is quite common today. However, the local loops at our homes, with few exceptions, are still analog. Eventually, all links and all networks of any kind (voice, video, data) will be digital, including the local loops. However, until a mad and/or prescient scientist finds a way to manipulate our genome, the final senders and receivers of information will remain analog, our mouths and ears.

Chapter 6

Bit Rates and
Broadband Networks

It is evident from the previous discussions that bandwidth is an important aspect of computer networks. Without bandwidth, the network user is dead in the networking water.

This chapter continues the discussions on bandwidth and revisits the concept of a broadband network. It examines how broadband networks can give network users better performance, mainly in reducing the time it takes to retrieve information from a network.

Also, the idea of a broadband local loop is explained. Don't forget, the local loop is the telephone and telephone wire (or wires) that connect our computer's modem to the outside world, to the Internet, for example. This arrangement is a big problem because the local loop does not provide much bandwidth.

This chapter also examines some new technologies (that you may be using) that are designed to increase the capacity of the local loops.

Response Time

In earlier chapters, we learned that the capacity of a network and a communications link is described in how many bits per second it can send and receive. The term bits per second is usually shortened to bps or bit/s.

We also saw that 7 or 8 bits make up a character, such as the letter J. These bits are also coded to form special control signals such as SYN or NAK.

We also know that the more bit/s the better, since a high bit rate results in faster transmissions and better response time. You can see the effect that bit rates have on your Web browsing. If you have a low-speed connection, it takes longer for a Web site to send a Web page to your computer. If you have a high-speed connection, the time is shorter, and you see the results on your screen sooner than with a low-speed connection.

It may be that you have a high-speed modem, but you still get a slow response to your query for a Web page. The reason is that the Internet may be congested. This term refers to the situation in which many people are logged on to the Internet at the same time. The switches and other machines in the network must queue email and Web requests and service them when they have an opportunity. It is the same situation when we go shopping during a busy time (say, just after work); the queues at the cash registers build up, and it takes longer to get service.

Thus, with slow modems or congested networks, the response to customers' service requests become longer. This concept is called *response time*, or in many situations, the lack of response time. One person said that www does not stand for World Wide Web, but for World Wide Wait. The reason is that we may have a very slow connection to the Internet, or the network may be congested. Whatever the situation, it is a big problem (but not necessarily the fault of the Web).

Examples of Bit Rates

Typical speeds of data communications systems are shown in Table 6.1. The table also explains commonly used terms. For example, 9600 bit/s is often shortened to 9.6 kbit/s (that is, 9.6 kilobit/s).

Table 6.1 Speeds and Uses

Typical Speeds in Bit/s	Typical Uses
0–600	Telegraph, older terminals; telemetry
600–9,600	Human-operated terminals; older modems
9,600–56,000	New modems (V.90, "56 kit/s")
64,000	Digital voice with ISDN
64,000–2,048,000	High speed for multiple users; computer-to-computer traffic; backbone links for networks; video
Greater than 2,048,000	Links for networks, high-quality video; multiple digital voice systems

The data communications world is fairly slow relative to the computer world. For example, a conventional data processing system with disk files attached to computers operates at millions of bits per second (Mbit/s) and up. A data communications system is slow because computers usually communicate through the telephone link, which was the most convenient and readily available path when the industry developed computers and began to interface the computers with terminals and other computers in the 1960s. The telephone channel is not designed for fast transmission between high-speed computers.

Notice the 64,000 bits per second rate in the table. This rate is for the digital voice capability described in Chapter 5.

The speeds that users usually obtain when they dial up and connect to the Internet are around 28 kbit/s to about 56 kbit/s. As mentioned earlier, the reasons for these transmission rates are due to the design of the dial-up telephone, the local loop, and the telephone plant at the telephone central office.

The speeds in the 64,000–2,048,000 bit/s range encompass offerings called dedicated (or leased) line products from the service providers (usually the telephone companies). A few arrangements are available for dial-up services in this bandwidth region. These systems are implemented with special equipment and software, both at the customer's site and the service provider's site. Since they provide more bandwidth, they are more expensive than the conventional dial-up service. You may be familiar with some of these offer-

conventional dial-up service. You may be familiar with some of these offerings; here are prominent examples, some of which are explained in more detail shortly:

- ❐ The Integrated Services Digital Network (ISDN)
- ❐ DS1 (also called T1 in some circles)
- ❐ Digital Subscriber Line (DSL)
- ❐ Cable modem

Broadband Systems Revisited

In most systems, the links and components (such as switches) within a network are of greater capacity than the links and components used by the network customer. Table 6.1 lists these offerings as the last entry with bit rates greater than 2,048,000. As Figure 6.1 shows, these high-speed links and switches are known as a *broadband network*.

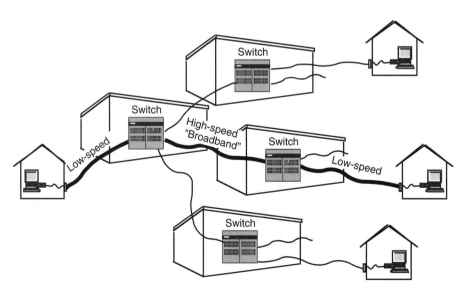

Figure 6.1   Broadband Networks

Most of these links are based on optical fiber. This technology is capable of transmitting very high bit rates, and some can send over 10,000,000,000 (giga) bits per second! Consequently, optical fiber is the preferred link technology in modern networks. Several vendors have optical fiber prototypes with a terabit (10^{12} bits per second) transmission capability. At this rate, a 1 Tbit/s fiber can transport just over 35 million data connections at 28.8 kbit/s, or about 17 million digital voice channels, or just under 500,000 compressed TV channels (or combinations of these channels).

Paraphrasing Thoreau once again, high-speed systems have nothing to do with the quality of their content. As things are going now, TV viewers can look forward to thousands of home shopping channels doing infomercials; or they can exercise some choice with the off button.

The Annoyance of Low Bandwidth Systems

Why can't all the links be high speed? Technically, they can. But the conventional telephone and the local loop, those wires that connect user computers to networks, are not designed to support high-capacity transmissions at high bit rates. These local loop wires are not optical fiber, but copper wire. It is not feasible to redesign the local loops throughout the world; think of the expense of pulling out all the copper wires from millions of homes and replacing it with optical fiber. So, with few exceptions, network users are stuck with the fairly low capacity (low bandwidth) links out of their homes and, to a lesser extent, their offices.

It can be quite an annoyance, especially when a user needs to transfer large files or to get a fast response from a query made to a network. The network itself may respond very quickly, but its response is often negated because of the slow local links that connect the user's computer to the network.

Relief in Sight

Ideally, users would like to have a broadband link from their computer to the network. This approach would translate into an end-to-end broadband capability, and it would also translate into a much more responsive system. Instead of waiting minutes for a response to a query to be sent to their computer, users would wait for a few seconds or even less.

Help is on the way. It is called by several names and is described shortly in this chapter.

The Network Cloud and the UNI

Before we further explore the issue of low-capacity and high-capacity systems, we need to digress a bit and examine Figure 6.2. The top part of the figure

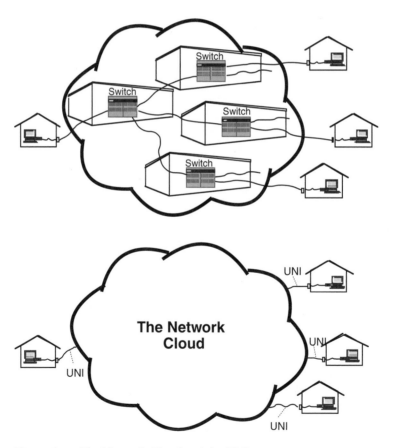

Figure 6.2   The Network Cloud and the UNI

shows the network inside a bubble, more commonly known as the *network cloud*. The individual components, such as links and switches, are shown within this cloud.

The bottom part of the figure does not show the details inside the network; it just assumes these components are there. This rendition of a network is used when it is not necessary to know about the details inside the network.

According to the network cloud idea, the emphasis is on the operations between the user and the network. Thus, the term "user network interface" (UNI) is used to describe this relationship.

Many of the operations that are important in data, voice, and video networks are performed at the UNI. Indeed, in many situations, the users of a network do not care about the operations inside the cloud. As long as the network transports the email between Ted and Bob correctly, and in a timely manner, the operations inside the network are of no concern to these individuals.

Broadband at the Local Loop: The Final Mile

The local loop is also called the final mile, denoting the last part of the telephone network connection to the customer. As noted earlier, help is on the way. Three new technologies are entering the market, and you may be using one of them now, purchased as a product from a telephone company, cable TV company, or perhaps a mobile phone company.

These technologies are being deployed now in most of the affluent cities in the world, and they all are classified as UNI technologies. That is, they operate between the user (customer) and the network (the network provider, such as the telephone company, an Internet Service Provider, etc.). Figure 6.3 shows three examples of these technologies.

These technologies support high bit rates. The rates vary, but most operate around 1,000,000 bits per second. Think of that! Instead of using a conventional 56,000 bit/s modem, we can avail ourselves of a new technology that is almost 20 times faster. It is no wonder that there are backlogs to get this service out to our homes and offices.

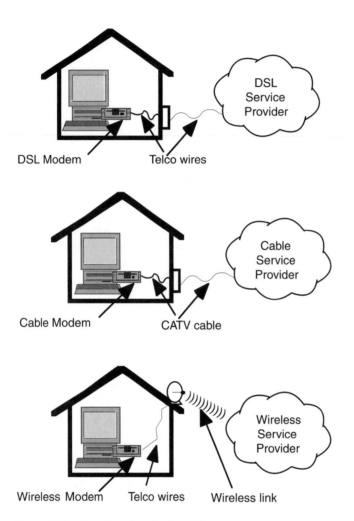

Figure 6.3   Broadband at the Local Loop

Here are their names and a brief description of their attributes. Once you buy one of these products, you will not want to go back to the old way of doing things.

❏ DSL (Digital Subscriber Line): This technology operates on the local loop owned by the telephone company but uses an advanced modem that is capable of very high bit rates. It is called a *DSL modem*. The telephone companies and their partners (some Internet Service Providers and some specialized firms) are offering DSL in most of the major cities in the industrialized world.

- ❑ Cable Modem: This technology uses the cable TV loops that have been installed for CATV. An advanced modem called a *cable modem* is also used. It too is capable of very high bit rates. As of this writing, the cable modem industry is even more popular than the DSL modem market.

- ❑ Wireless Local Loops: This technology is an extension of the conventional wireless media. Some implementations use cell phones, but they are not capable of high bit rates. Other implementations use special methods to achieve high bit rates. This technology has great potential, but it is not a big market as of this writing.

The companies who are providing these services compete with each other for our business. It is unlikely that you will subscribe to more than one of these offerings, since they are somewhat redundant in what they do: give you more bandwidth.

And they may not be available in your neighborhood. For example, I cannot get any of these services at my home; I live in the country and consider myself fortunate to have a local loop to the telephone office. If I need to do a lot of work on the Internet, I work from other locations.

Summary

Bandwidth is one of the most important components of computer networks. In this chapter we examined how broadband networks can provide better performance, both in response time and throughput.

The problem with the local loop was explained, and we learned that it does not have much bandwidth. The chapter concluded with a look at some new technologies to increase the capacity of the local loops, principally DSL, cable modems, and the upcoming data over wireless technologies.

One of the big issues in the United States regarding the local loop and the cable TV plant is that these precious facilities are privately owned by the local telephone companies and the cable TV companies, respectively. These owners are understandably reluctant to share their property with other companies, who are potential competitors for their customers. To paraphrase the old adage, "Not with my wire, you don't!"

Those who wish to use these facilities claim the telephone companies and the cable operators are not motivated to upgrade their final mile to broadband because they have little competition for these local services. They also claim that the rights to build the final mile facilities were granted to them by the U.S. government as part of a regulated monopoly approach to a limited resource.

Both sides have merits to their arguments. If I were one of these owners, I am sure I would say, "Stay away from my wire." If I were a potential competitor, I would want access to the wire.

Chapter 7

Voice and Data Characteristics

This chapter explains why voice and data traffic are different from each other. After having read the last few chapters of this book, you may question my last statement. After all, if voice and data are simply coded into a bunch of bits, then both are merely composed of 1s and 0s. True, but there is more to the story than binary digits, and we will examine the rest of it here.

Other new concepts are introduced. One is the notion of *real-time* traffic; another is *bursty* traffic; and the last is the *packet*.

Voice Requirements

Thus far in the analysis of communications networks, we have not spent a great deal of time discussing the differences between voice and data networks. For the first few chapters, several examples showed how voice and data operations take place, but the discussions have been somewhat general.

We now examine in more detail these two kinds of networks, because there is a great difference in how they operate. The difference rests on the fact that voice networks must support *real-time* interactions between two communicating parties, and data networks do not (with rare exceptions) have this requirement imposed on them.

Real-Time Needs

The term real time was coined in the 1960s to denote a situation in which events happen very fast. When Ted says hello, this greeting is passed through the telephone network to Bob almost instantaneously, as shown in Figure 7.1.

The network is not allowed to tarry; it must present the hello to Bob as soon as possible. Why is this so? Because a voice network is designed to make delay imperceptible between the two conversing parties, regardless of the locations.

Consider the telephone network design: Ted and Bob may be located in distant parts of the planet; their conversations may traverse thousands of miles and the hello may be transported through scores of components (such as switches). Yet the network provides such fast response time that Ted and Bob may think they are next door to each other.

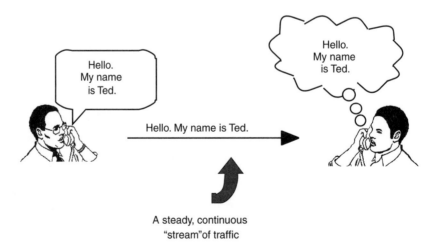

Figure 7.1   Voice Flow

The Need for Continuous Bandwidth

There is another important aspect to voice transmissions. They must be continuous between the speaker and the listener. Recall that most voice signals are now converted to digital bits of 1s and 0s. They are then sent on to the link in discrete time slots, an idea explained in Chapter 5, Figure 5.3. These time slots must be sent in a continuous fashion. They are not allowed to be stored somewhere in the network and then sent at a later time.

Imagine if delays did happen in the network. The "Hello. This is Ted." greeting might arrive something like this: Hello......(a few seconds of delay)......This is......(a few more seconds of delay)......Ted.

Needless to say, this is not a very effective way to communicate.

Thus, voice traffic expects the network to provide a continuous (constant) supply of bandwidth, in order to prevent the unacceptable "bursty" service just explained. This idea is called *constant bit rate (CBR)*. As shown next, CBR services are just the opposite of what data traffic needs.

Data Requirements

Consider data networks. When Ted types the email message to Bob, there is no notion of "real time." Indeed, Ted often creates the message and stores it for later transmittal. Even if Ted sends the email as soon as he types it into the computer, it is not a big deal if the email arrives in a non-real-time mode. That is, if it is delayed a few seconds in the network, it is not perceptible to Bob. It may even be delayed for minutes, hours, or days, depending on how Bob chooses to open and read his email file.

Furthermore, in Figure 7.2, Bob is not at his computer, so the need for quick delivery of the email is not an issue. Even if Bob had his computer turned on, a few seconds delay in the delivery of the message is not perceptible. After all, Bob does not know when (or even if) Ted sent the email!

In a chat room session, users interact by sending messages to each other. This session is a data session and requires faster response time than does an

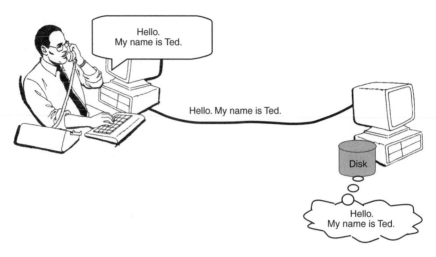

Figure 7.2 Data Flow

off-line email delivery. But it is still not real time. The delay between the time one person keys in a message and when it is received by the chat room partner can be several seconds. A lapse of several seconds may seen like a very short time to humans, but it is a very long time in the view of computers and computer networks.

Data is "Bursty"

Another aspect to consider is that many data transfers entail the downloading of a file from a disk or computer memory. The accesses to the disk or computer memory to retrieve the data take time. During these accesses, the communications channel is not being used.

Referring to Figure 7.3, Bob is going to reply to Ted, but not immediately, so Bob has stored his email to Ted on a disk file for sending at a later time. His response is a laconic "OK, my name is Bob."

When it is time to send the message (Bob later instructs the computer to send the message), there will be periods of activity and inactivity on the communications link, as the message is accessed from the disk (or computer mem-

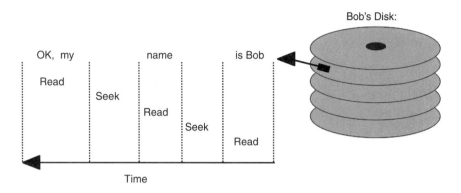

Figure 7.3   Another Look at Data Characteristics

ory). The time spent by the disk unit reading the file, the transfer of the data from the disk to the computer, and then on to the communications link means there will be times when the link is waiting for the message to be sent.

Thus, data communications are said to be bursty. The term means that most data transmissions have periods when the communications link is used (a burst of traffic), and periods when the link is empty, or inactive (a "no burst"). This concept is called *variable bit rate (VBR)*.

Another example of bursty data transmissions is a typist keying characters on a keyboard and sending them on to a data network. The keying-in style is very erratic, very bursty.

The Effect of the Bursty Process on the Communications Link

The result of the bursty disk input/output (I/O) operations or the bursty typing translates to bursty (that is, VBR) transmissions on the communications link, as shown in Figure 7.4. Again, notice that there are times when the communications link is not being used; it is temporarily idle (inactive).

There is another aspect to data traffic that has not been discussed. For large transmissions involving thousands of bits, the payload is split into smaller

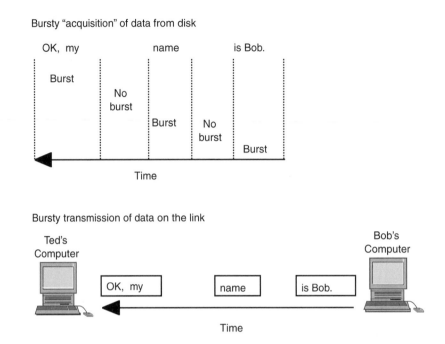

Figure 7.4 Effect on Traffic Patterns

pieces. In our email example, if either Bob or Ted keys in a long message or sends a large file, the data is usually separated into these pieces.

Several reasons exist why a large user payload is divided. One reason is that the computer may not wait for (say) Ted to enter the entire message before sending it; after all, Ted may be a slow typist. The computer may send pieces, perhaps after Ted has entered a sentence and pressed Return on the computer keyboard. The Return key function could be a way of informing the computer to transmit what Ted has entered to that point.

As discussed previously, noise on the link may create errors (damaging a few bits) in the payload. When this happens, the entire payload may be present. So, if the payload is small, fewer bits are retransmitted than if the payload were large. This approach makes better use of the link's bandwidth.

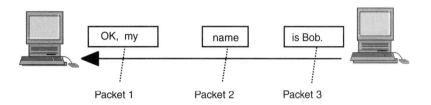

Figure 7.5 Packets

The Packet

The three pieces of data that were sent from Ted to Bob in Figure 7.4 are known by various names in the data communications industry. The most common name is *packet*. In Figure 7.5, three packets are sent across the link.

The term packet originated in the British data communications industry in the late 1960s to denote a small unit of traffic on a data link. I suppose most people associate the term packet with something small. I do. I think of a packet as a small parcel or bundle of something. In this example, the packet is a small bundle of bits.

And Self-Containment

The British engineers also defined the packet as being self-contained and independent of any other packets in the data network. Really? It seems that the three packets in the example are very closely related. After all, one packet is rather meaningless without the others. So, what is true: are they related or not?

The answer is that Ted's and Bob's chat and email applications (and others, such as file transfer) certainly think of these three packets as being related to each other. After all, if packet 2 does not arrive at the receiving computer, Ted will read on his screen, "OK, my is Bob." The sentence leaves a lot to the imagination.

The communications network (and not the user application) considers the packets as being independent of each other. To this network, they are nothing more than a bundle, or packet, of bits. In fact, the network doesn't even know what the bits mean. The bits could be the email in the example, a funds transfer to a bank, a credit card payment, a stock quote, anything.

How to Deliver? Use an Address in the Packet Header

Then how can these self-contained packets be delivered correctly between Ted and Bob? Just like the post office does: with an *address*. The job of the network is to deliver the bits safely to the receiving user by using an *address* in a part of the packet called the *packet header*.

The packet header is a new idea, and it has not been shown in any of the previous figures. We must hold these thoughts for later parts of this book (Chapter 9), and when we return to them, I will point you back to this part of the material.

Summary

In Chapter 5, we learned that voice and data traffic can be sent as 1s and 0s. Nonetheless, in this chapter we learned that the network performance requirements for voice and data are quite different:

- ❐ Voice needs real-time response and constant bandwidth—a CBR service.
- ❐ Data does not need real-time response and can function with bursty (variable) bandwidth—a VBR service.

To summarize some key ideas of this chapter, Bob's computer has composed a poem for the network:

My buffer is full,
your link is free.
I need some help
with my packets three.
So, take my bit and smack it
into your next available packet.

The composer (who shall remain anonymous) of this awful verse offers apologies to a songwriter named Johnny Paycheck (from which the stanza was borrowed), who wrote a famous song for disaffected programmers in which he sang, "Take this bit and stuff it, I ain't writing code no more."[1] Mr. Paycheck's rendition is considerably different, but the idea is intact.

---

1. This pun might be appreciated more by some of the Networking 102 readers, who have dealt with bit stuffing in a payload to prevent certain bit sequences (such as NAK) from appearing in the user bit stream.

Chapter 8

Multiplexing and Packet Switching

This chapter continues the discussion of the bursty transmission characteristics of data. It explains how this aspect of data traffic might lead to wasted capacity (wasted bandwidth) in the network, resulting in higher costs to the network service provider and to the network customer.

The chapter also introduces the concept of multiplexing, a method for using the expensive communications network facilities in a much more efficient manner, resulting in lower costs to all. The chapter concludes with an introduction of a network machine that combines the multiplexing function with the switching function; the machine is called a *packet switch*.

Idle Bandwidth = Wasted Capacity

Let's have another look at the data transmission from Bob to Ted as depicted in Figure 8.1.

The bursty packets have not consumed all the bandwidth on the link. The notations "Wasted Capacity" show that extra bandwidth is available for the two users if they have something else to send to each other. But in this exam-

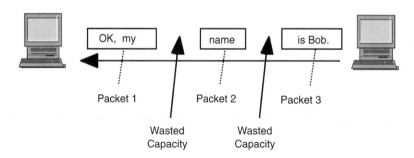

OK, my   name   is Bob.

Packet 1   Packet 2   Packet 3

Wasted   Wasted
Capacity   Capacity

Figure 8.1   Inefficient Use of the Link

ple, they do not. Consequently, the communications link is not being used to its full capacity.

This situation is undesirable. Links are expensive; they are physical wires or wireless systems. They require switches, special power supplies, buildings, and so forth that cost a lot of money to design, build, install, and maintain. Installation is especially expensive because it is labor-intensive: digging trenches for the wires, laying the wires, erecting the towers for the wireless antenna, etc. The network service providers such as AT&T, Level 3, etc. want to put as much payload traffic as possible on the links in the network to increase revenue. This example depicts an operation that is not very attractive to the service provider (and the company's stockholders).

Nor is it attractive to the customers of the service, because it means each customer may be paying for the entire bandwidth of the link, when only part of the bandwidth is being used.

The Solution Is Multiplexing

There is a solution to this problem. The common-sense approach is to place other users' payload on the links in the network. In Figure 8.2, two other network users have been added, Carol and Alice. They too are sending email messages to each other.

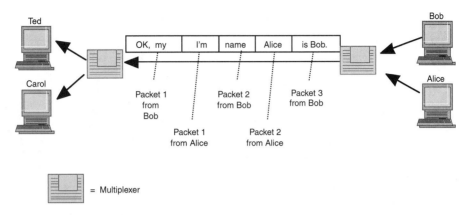

Figure 8.2 Improving Link Efficiency

We can see that the configuration has been changed. Another machine has been added to the topology. It is called a *multiplexer,* and it enables more than one set of users to share the communications link. The multiplexer is also called a *MUX.*

The MUX provides a very powerful service both for network providers and network customers by enabling the sharing of the resources of network links. For the provider, more payload can be supported by the network, which results in greater revenue. For the customer, the cost of operating the network by the provider decreases, with these savings passed on to the customers (the customers hope). And Bob, Carol, Ted, and Alice are sharing yet another resource.[1]

Multiplexers accept lower-speed voice or data signals from terminals, telephones, and user applications and combine them into one high-speed stream for transmission onto a link. A receiving multiplexer demultiplexes and converts the combined stream into the original multiple lower-speed signals. Since several separate transmissions are sent over the same link, the efficiency of the link is improved.

---

1. For the reader who does not know about the cult movie made in 1969 called *Bob & Carol & Ted & Alice,* check it out from your video store. It's an entertaining story about other aspects of resource sharing.

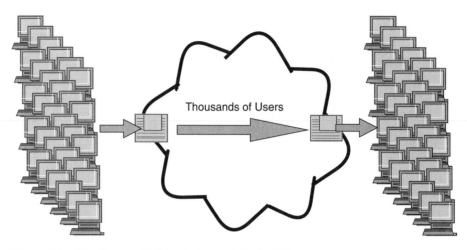

Figure 8.3   The Power of Multiplexing and Optical Fiber

Thousands of Users on One Link

Recall that the links inside the network (inside the network cloud) are usually high-capacity optical fiber, whereas the links connecting the user to the network are plain old, low-capacity copper wire.

As depicted in Figure 8.3, the multiplexers are placed at the "edge" of a communications network (the network cloud), both at the entrance to and exit from the network. Each user is connected to the multiplexer through the user's local loop (once again, the copper). From there, the multiplexer combines many users' traffic onto one (or a few) optical fibers for transport through the network to the exit to the network, that is, the exit multiplexer. Here the situation is reversed: the multiplexed traffic is demultiplexed and sent to each user on the individual copper wires.

How Many Users?

Thousands of users on one optical fiber (or a few fibers) is a lot of users. Just how many users this may be can be understood with some simple math. Chapter 5 explained the idea of digital voice. Recall that Ted's or Bob's digital voice consists of 64,000 bits per second: eight thousand 8-bit samples (8,000 × 8 = 64,000) are transmitted.

In North America, one of the popular fiber networks used by the traditional telephone companies and other companies such as Level 3 and Quest to transport telephone calls is based on multiplexing telephone traffic onto optical fibers. This system is capable of supporting almost 130,000 simultaneous 64 kbit/s phone calls on one fiber.

And this system is far from being "state of the art." Systems being developed today have orders of magnitude more bandwidth. If only we could get a fraction of this type of capacity onto the local loop to our homes.

Combining the Multiplexer and the Switch: The Packet Switch

At this point, it is appropriate to introduce another powerful weapon to the networking arsenal and to add another piece to the Networking 101 puzzle. This piece is called the *packet switch*. As shown in Figure 8.4, the packet switch multiplexes many users onto one high-speed link, say, the links from San Diego to Chicago, and San Diego to Dallas.

The packet switch can also switch traffic by placing the packet on the link to Chicago or on an alternate link to Dallas. For example, assume that Ted is located in San Diego and his computer is connected to a packet switch in that city. Bob is located in Chicago and is also connected to a packet switch in that area.

When Ted sends his email to Bob, the packet switch is smart enough to know to send the email's packets onto the link from San Diego to Chicago, and not the link from San Diego to Dallas. The second choice is not very efficient, since it means sending the traffic though an extra "hop," the packet switch in Dallas.

How can the packet switch know how to relay the traffic to the Chicago node and not the Dallas node? As introduced in Chapter 7, the packet switch examines another piece of information in the packet. It is called an address and is explained in the next chapter.

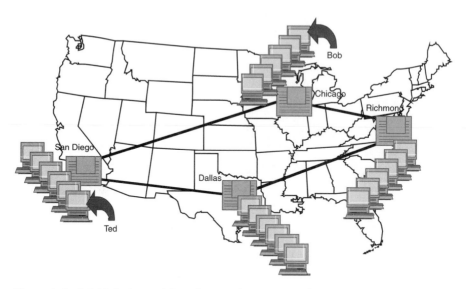

Figure 8.4   Multiplexing and Switching in the Same Machine: The Packet Switch

Summary

This chapter introduced the concept of multiplexing, a common-sense, yet powerful, method for using the expensive communications network facilities in a much more efficient manner. The machine that performs these functions is called a multiplexer. The chapter concluded with the introduction of another machine, called a packet switch, that combines the multiplexing function with the switching function.

Chapter 9

Network IDs: Addresses

For network users to communicate with each other, they must have some means of identification. This situation holds for other systems, such as the postal service and the telephone system.

In this chapter, another piece of the Networking 101 puzzle is examined, a network identifier (ID), specifically called a *network address*. The chapter also explains the well-known and widely used network address (which all Internet users use when they log on to the Internet), called the IP address.

Postal Addresses and Network Addresses

The postal service uses addresses such as street names, house numbers, cities, states, and ZIP codes for identifiers. In computer networks, the method to relay email is similar to postal mail: a destination address is examined by the relaying entity (for this explanation, a packet switch; for the postal service, a mail person). This address determines how the packet switch or mail person forwards the data packet or the mail envelope to the final recipient. The computer network's "post office" is the email server; see scenario 4 in Appendix A.

In Figure 9.1, the postal address is 188 Anystreet, Anywhere 88888. The ID of "Bob" is not an address per se. That is, the postal service will not deliver the envelope based on "Bob." There are some exceptions: the names of Santa Claus, the President of the United States, and a few others, are indeed delivered to preestablished locations.

In this example, the computer network address is 192 (a generic address, for simplicity; we will worry about the details later). This address is Bob's address. Ted or Ted's computer is responsible for placing this address in the packet or

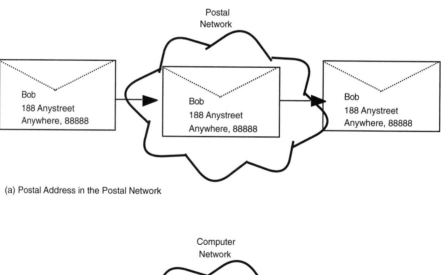

(a) Postal Address in the Postal Network

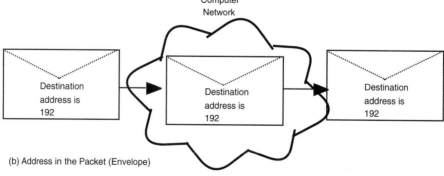

(b) Address in the Packet (Envelope)

Figure 9.1   Addresses

packets that are sent to Bob or Bob's server. In Figure 9.1(b), the packet is called an envelope in order to correlate the example to the postal service term.

Keep in mind that the packet has two parts: (a) the packet header and (b) the packet payload. In the mail analogy, the packet header can be thought of as the envelope, and the packet payload is the letter inside the envelope.

The Address in the Packet Header

As depicted in Figure 9.2, the structure of the packet is now a bit different; it contains an address. In fact, *each* packet for this specific email transmission contains the address of the destination user. This address is placed in a special part of the packet, which we now know is called the packet header. This header is not considered part of the user payload, but it is used to support the payload.

Packet Independence and Envelope Independence

Perhaps it is now evident why earlier descriptions called the packet self-contained. Each packet in this email (there are two packets in this example) contains the destination address of the email recipient or the recipient's email server. As a consequence, the packets are not dependent on each other for their transport through the network; the address gives each packet a unique identification. In this example, the IDs (the addresses) are the same, but if packets are going to different destinations, the addresses are different.

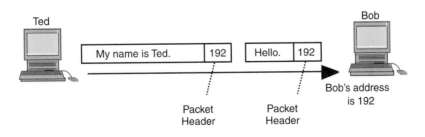

Figure 9.2 The Address and the Packet Header

Routing the Mail Envelope and Routing the Packet

As explained in more detail in a later chapter, each packet in the email example may even take a different route through the network. After all, each packet has its own address. This operation is exactly like the postal service.

The communications network and the postal service consider each packet and each envelope to be completely independent. If I were to write you a long letter that would not fit into one postal envelope, I might place the letter in two envelopes. The postal service treats the two envelopes separately.

Just like packets in a communications network, the two postal envelopes may take different routes through the postal system to the mail recipient. And like a packet network, the two letters may arrive out of order. And like the packet network the letters may not arrive (of course, they usually do).

But I am getting slightly ahead of myself, and in this chapter, the subject is addresses. Routing is explained in a later chapter.

The IP Address

The network address emphasized in this book is called the *Internet Protocol (IP)* address (see Figure 9.3). Other address plans are used in computer networks, but the IP address is prevalent, so it is highlighted. The previous example of network address 192 was an example only and not based on the IP formal addressing plan. The IP address is made up of three identifiers (IDs):[1]

❑ Network: An ID of a network, such as AOL, in the public Internet; a private internet/intranet, such as a network inside a company's building; or on a private campus.

---

1. Some networks do not use three notations, but combine some of them. For the *Networking 102* reader, you probably know this approach by the terms address aggregation and subnetting. Also, other IDs are often used in telephone and data networks, such as a country code for dialing to another country. These details are not important to our basic discussions.

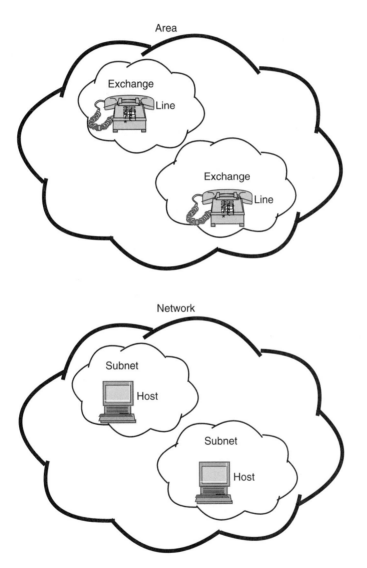

Figure 9.3   Addressing Plans

❏ Subnetwork: An ID of a network operating within another network, just defined. The term *sub* implies an addressing hierarchy. It does not mean a subnetwork is not a fully functioning network. A good way to look at this idea is that several subnetworks may be associated with a network. By using the Network ID, we could refer to all the subnetworks. By using the Subnet ID, we could refer to one of them. As we will see shortly, this idea gives the network manager a lot of flexibility in determining how packets are sent through a network. By the way, a subnetwork is usually called a subnet.

❏ Host: An ID of the end-user's device, such as a PC, a palm device, a workstation, etc. This host ID is associated with the subnet address ID, so it implies that the host is connected to the subnet that is identified in the subnet part of the address. For example, if a packet is to be sent to Chicago, the packet address will contain the host ID and the subnet (and network ID, of course) to which that PC is connected.

Network ID/Subnet ID/Host ID Is Like Area Code/Exchange Code/Line Number

This three-part aspect of network addressing can be confusing to the newcomer, but we have been using this concept for many years with the plain old telephone service (POTS).

The IP addressing plan can be compared to the telephone number, but keep in mind that the two addressing plans are not designed to be exchangeable, although some networks have a service that allows a user to correlate an IP address with a phone number. Anyway, here is a comparison of the IP address to the telephone number.

❏ The telephone 3-digit area code is similar to the IP address Network ID.

❏ The telephone 3-digit exchange code is similar to the IP address Subnet ID.

❏ The telephone 4-digit line number is similar to the IP address Host ID.

The Hierarchical Addresses

Both addressing plans are hierarchical. That is, to reach a user in a telephone system or an Internet, a system first looks at the area code/Network ID, then the exchange code/Subnetwork ID, and then the line number/Host ID.

In a telephone network, the dialed number is used by the telephone offices (and the telephone switches, see Chapter 6, Figure 6.1) to route the call to the called party. In a data network, the IP address is used by the Internet (and the packet switches, see Chapter 8, Figure 8.4) to route packets to the destination party.

But We May Not Enter a Network Address

So far so good. But there is one small problem. When users log on to a data network, like the Internet, it is likely that they never enter an address. Instead, users enter something like *uyless@infoinst.com* or click on an entry in a page on the computer screen that looks like uyless@infoinst.com. Perhaps it looks like www.uyless@infoinst.com. The point is that the rather cryptic network ID, subnet ID, and host ID are not entered.

The Email Address vs. the Network Address

It is also likely that you have been calling notations like uyless@infoinst.com an email address. A logical question is where does this email address fit in with the network address?

I ask for your patience about this important matter. Let's finish the analysis of the network address in this chapter. Then, in the next chapter, we will examine those www.uyless@infoinst.com notations. Also, in the next chapter we will tie together the network address and the so-called email address.

The IP Addressing Standard

Internets use a 32-bit address to identify a host computer and the network/subnet to which the host is attached. The structure of the IP address is depicted in Figure 9.4. Its format is:

IP address = Network ID + Subnet ID + Host ID

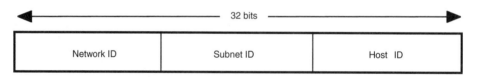

Figure 9.4   The IP Address

The IP address identifies a host's connection to its subnetwork. Consequently, if a host machine is moved to another subnetwork, its address must be changed.

IP addresses are classified by their formats, and several formats are permitted. The format layouts describe how many of the 32 bits are used for the network, subnet, and host IDs. We need not concern ourselves with all these formats in Networking 101; we will leave those details to Networking 102.

Difficulty of Dealing with 32-Bit Numbers

A 32-bit binary number is quite difficult to read. For easier viewing of the address, the 32 bits are divided into four 8-bit octets and are depicted as four decimal equivalents. So, the 8-bit octet of 00000011 is displayed in the Internet documentation as a decimal 3. Figure 9.5 shows these ideas.

The result of this practice is that the four decimal numbers are then separated by periods (called "dots") to delineate them from each other, as in 192.75.88.5.

At first glance, this idea can be a bit tricky. What happened to the hierarchical addresses of the three IDs? Looking at the four decimal values, it might be assumed that there are four IDs. That is not the case. Remember that this decimal notation is used for ease of reading and ease of reference. For example, if I were to give someone my IP address, it is a lot easier to say, "My address is 192 dot 75 dot 88 dot 5," than to recite a string of thirty two 1s and 0s.

The key to understanding this concept is to visualize that the Network ID, the Subnet ID, and the Host ID simply span these 32 bits. The number of bits allocated to each of them depends on the overall composition of the network, the subnets, and the hosts.

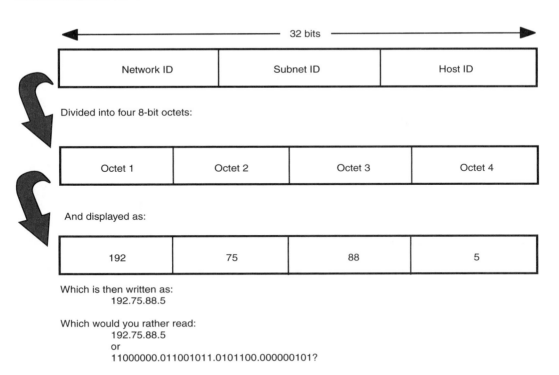

Figure 9.5 Address Conventions

The Ultimate Purpose of the IP Address

The details of how many bits make up a Host ID and so forth are not important to us at this part of our learning process. What is of paramount importance is to understand that the purpose of the IP address is (a) to identify the destination of the packet and (b) to allow a packet switch to examine this address in order to relay the packet to this destination.

If you understand these two aspects of the IP address, anything else is not as important; it's frosting on the cake.

Summary

The postal service uses addresses for identifiers in order to route mail to the receiving party. So does the telephone network. In computer networks, the method is the same. The address is called a network address, and it is used by packet switches to route the packets to the receiving party.

The structure of the famous IP address is similar to a conventional telephone number. Both contain three parts, and both allow a telephone switch or a packet switch to forward telephone calls and IP packets, respectively.

Computer networks usually route user packets to their proper destination without error, but there are occasions when packets may be lost. The reasons vary. Some losses occur because of faulty addresses; others occur because of faulty operations at a packet switch. Some people call these circumstances the "black hole." No one knows what happens to the packets until some trouble-shooting operations take place.

Other networks have their black holes. Several years ago, U.S. postal authorities discovered that a major mail exchange office in Northern Virginia had loads of old mail stored in some old trucks at the back of the facility. It so happens that this exchange provides services to my home.

I would like to have had the capability of routing my mail around this faulty exchange, as we can do in computer networks. Unfortunately, I was relegated to tell my creditors, "The check is in the mail, but it may be in a postal black hole." I liked the explanation, it had a sense of mystery to it. My creditors were not impressed.

Chapter **10**

Network IDs: Names

This chapter introduces the second form of a network ID, a *network name*. The purpose of a network name is explained, and network names are compared to network addresses, explained in Chapter 9. This chapter also introduces another network component, and another piece to the Networking 101 puzzle, the *name server*.

This chapter also makes the point that a network name is also called an *email address* by many people. In some networks the network name is called a *screen name*.

The last part of the chapter shows how the network names for Ted and Bob can be correlated with their network addresses.

The subject of network names is divided into two chapters. After you read this chapter, you might want to page ahead and take a look at Chapter 15. But it is not necessary; the chapters are presented in a logical order, and Chapter 15 is in the right sequence.

The Network Name Is Not an Address

As noted, another identifier used in many networks is a name. A name is not an address. It does not have any location significance, such as a network ID or an area code. Quite the contrary, names are intended to have *no* location significance. Part of their intent is to be independent of any geographical constraint.

In Figure 10.1, the postal address is on an envelope. It actually has an address and a name. The address is street number, street, city, and state. The name Bob is the recipient of the mail on the other part of the envelope.

As noted in Chapter 9, if an envelope is sent with only a name on it, it is not going to be delivered. If it is sent with the address, it will be delivered to that address. (Of course, it might not be opened or it might be thrown away, but it will be delivered to the address on the envelope.)

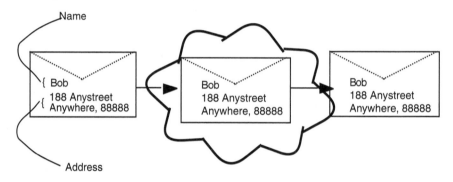

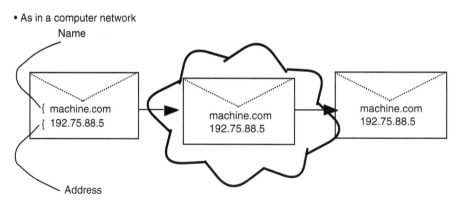

Figure 10.1   Network Names

Flexibility of the Network Name

Furthermore, if Uyless Black has a hypothetical network name, say, uyless.com (I'll explain the .com in a later chapter), he can have mail delivered to him at different addresses. So can a computer. Let's assume a computer has a hypothetical network name of machine.com. It can have email delivered to it at different addresses. You probably do this often if you have a laptop PC and are a traveler. Assume you are traveling and you go from your home to a hotel. You may be moving (connecting) to a different network in the Internet.

   Unbeknown to you, your computer and the new network exchange information to use different network addresses to support your mobility. However, it is entirely possible for you to keep the same Internet name (such as my uyless.com or the PC's machine.com) while you use alternate connections to the two networks, the one associated with your residence and the one associated with the hotel.

Figure 10.1 uses the postal service analogy from earlier chapters to show the relationships of mail names and addresses to their counterparts in computer networks. For this figure, keep one point in mind. In the postal service, there is always supposed to be a name and an address on the envelope. In a computer network, the name is usually carried inside the packet (the payload), and the address is carried in the packet header. Here is the comparison:

Postal Service:	Name: on the envelope	Address: on the envelope
Network:	Name: in the payload	Address: in the packet header

Moving Around and Keeping the Same Name

As noted, one advantage to the network name concept is that a name, once assigned, can be associated with the entity (say, a person, a network, or even a computer) with which it is identified, regardless of where the entity goes. As we just learned, if a machine is assigned a name of machine.com, this name can belong to this machine indefinitely, even though the machine may be moved from one network to another. Of course, if it is moved to another network, then it usually must give up the use of the old network ID, that is, its network address.

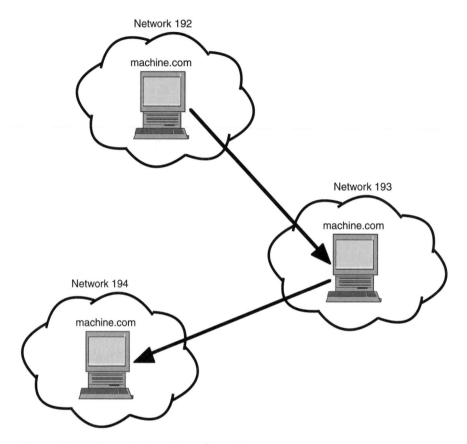

Figure 10.2   Name: Independent of Location

So, machine.com might be identified with network 192, because it is indeed connected to this network. However, if the machine moves to network 193, shown in Figure 10.2, it must shed the old network address and take on the new address. Fortunately, Ted and Bob do not have to worry about these address changes because the network automatically handles the changes.

To summarize, one attractive aspect of using a name is that network users are no longer bound by a restrictive address and can move into and out of different networks and subnetworks and keep their own names.

There are some exceptions to this summary. For example, my company has a name of infoinst.com (for Information Engineering Institute), and it is independent of any network affiliation. I also have a name that is associated with aol.com. If I log on to, say, mindspring.net, I cannot use my aol.com name; I use the Mindspring name. However, I can still move about and use these names. For example, I use my aol.com name in many countries in Europe, and my friends and associates always know me by that name. It is AOL's job to keep track of me and make known to these people which of AOL's subnets I am connected to.

Figure 10.2 shows that machine.com moves to three different networks (or subnetworks that are associated with a network), but its name is still machine.com.

Is It infoinst.com, INFOINST.com, or InfoInst.com?

You may have noticed that sometimes the network name is written as upper case and sometimes lower case, or even combinations of the two. In the past, some implementations of the network name were case sensitive, and in others, they were not. I am not a very good typist and I sometimes enter a network name differently with regard to upper or lower case letters. Most of the time, my entry is accepted, but it is a good idea to enter the name exactly as it was given to you. Lately, I have had no problem with case sensitivity.

But Isn't the Network Name an Email Address?

In Chapter 9, I noted that you may not type an address, but something like uyless@infoinst.com. Part of this entry represents a network name, but it is more commonly known as an *email address*. Therefore, an email address is really not an address; it is a name. But most of us say something like, "Here is my email address." I do it all the time. Just know that you are conveying your network name, and not an address.

We are close to filling in a very important piece of our Networking 101 puzzle: the ability to relate a network name (all right! an email address) to a network address.

A Vital Network Component: The Name Server

Keeping the name independent of a location but then associating it with a location-dependent address as needed is a powerful concept. Location-independent names support the idea of mobility, an important part of our lives. Central to this idea is this: a person, such as Ted, does not need to know the address of someone else, such as Bob, to send a message to that person. All Ted needs to know is Bob's network name (assume it is bob.com).

Bob can move practically anywhere, and Ted neither knows nor cares where Bob is located, because Ted does not have to keep track of Bob's address.

But someone or something must know how to associate the name to the address, and that something is known as a name server. Its job is to store the name of bob.com *and* associate an address with the name. The address is then used to relay (route) the traffic to Bob through packet switches that understand addresses and how to relay the packets to those destinations, a subject for a later chapter.

You may be wondering why this concept is so grand. After all, there must still be an association of the name to the address. Yes, but Ted does not have to do it. It is relegated to the name server. And the name server's job is just that: to correlate a name to its appropriate address.

Email and Other Forms of Messages

We must now make a slight alteration to our mail scenario. To do so, we distinguish between email and other forms of messaging. The next part of this chapter uses an instant messaging example. Here are the salient differences between these operations.

> ❐ With email, Ted's traffic to Bob is sent to a designated mail server for Bob. Later, Bob can log on to his network and access this mail server to obtain his mail. In this scenario, a name server can be used to provide the address of the mail server, and Ted's packets will have the address of the mail server in the packet header.

❏ With some other forms of messaging, the packets are sent directly between Ted and Bob. For example, newer systems do not use a server, and allow the messages to flow directly between the users' computers. Examples are the well-known H.323 endpoint-to-endpoint option, and Yahoo's instant message system.

In the example in Figure 10.3, when Ted types in "bob.com," Ted's computer sends a special packet to an established name server. This packet does not contain user traffic. It is a special packet, called a query packet. Its contents are coded to ask the server if it knows the network address of bob.com (or other users, such as alice.com).

In the example, the server sends back a response to Ted's computer, stating that bob.com can be reached by the IP address of 192.75.88.5.

These activities take place very quickly, usually in a fraction of a second—so quickly that Ted does not know his computer and the server are doing this work on his behalf.

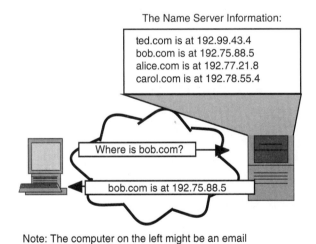

The Name Server Information:

ted.com is at 192.99.43.4
bob.com is at 192.75.88.5
alice.com is at 192.77.21.8
carol.com is at 192.78.55.4

Where is bob.com?

bob.com is at 192.75.88.5

Note: The computer on the left might be an email
server or other type of server

Figure 10.3   The Name Server

One more point about this wonderful service. The information obtained from the name server is usually stored inside Ted's computer. Consequently, the next time Ted sends an instant message to Bob, the needed IP address is already available at Ted's computer and the query and response packets do not have to be sent to and from the name server. This approach is just one way of reducing overhead traffic in a network.

The Email Server and the Name Server

For email, the terminal (PC) depicted in Figure 10.3 is not an end user machine, but a mail server. Therefore, the mail server is communicating with the name server, and not the user machine. However, some systems are set up for the user machine to interact directly with the name server. Some private networks place their name server operations in a local router, one that is attached to the private network. Other computers, routers, and servers can then use this router for name-to-address resolution.

Name Servers Support Thousands of Users

A name server provides its services to hundreds of thousands of people. This approach makes it unnecessary for Bob, Carol, Ted, Alice, you, me, and so forth to have to remember all those decimal digits of an address.

Just consider: when you want to send packets to someone, must you enter a 32-bit address or even a 4-octet address? No, all you need to do is enter a name, such as bob.com. What a hassle it would be if all of us had to remember and type addresses every time we wanted to send an email or an instant message.

It is a big job to keep these records up-to-date and correct. So whose job is it?

In private networks, an individual or a project team is responsible for entering the name/address record into the name server database. Usually, a new employee is given these IDs during the first few days of employment.

For public networks, the job of associating a name to an address is usually given to the Internet Service Provider (ISP), such as AOL, MSN, and so on. If you want to have your own unique network name, you can certainly get one registered to you for a small fee. Chapter 15 provides more information on this topic.

A Review of the Concepts

There is another aspect to names that warrants review. A name and an address are usually associated with a machine or a person. It is easier to use a name than an address. For example, if you were typing a message to Bob, which ID would you prefer to key in (as well as remember)?

❑ Option A: bob.com
❑ Option B: 192.75.88.5

Next, Routing the Packet

After the name server has presented Ted's computer (or Ted's server) with Bob's address, the computer places this address in the packet header, as shown in Figure 10.4. Ted again need not be concerned about this operation, for it is done automatically by a piece of software in the computer. The payload in the packet of course contains the user's traffic.

The address is then used by the switches to route the packet through the network, eventually to Bob. So, once again, it is analogous to the postal service or the telephone network.

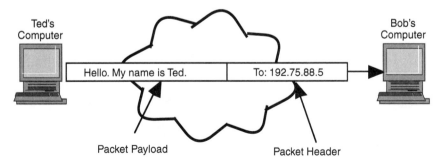

Figure 10.4 Then, Using the Address, the Packet is Routed to Bob

In Figure 10.4, the full message of "Hello. My name is Ted." is sent in one packet. Remember that only part of the message may reside in the packet. As noted earlier, the first packet may be "Hello.", with the packet header placed in front of this payload. Subsequent packets would then contain the remainder of the message, and each packet payload has a packet header containing the destination address.

The Name Server Is Like a Telephone Directory

Here are some analogies to the computer network name server. We can think of the telephone directory as a name server. After all, it associates names with addresses. Some of us even have our telephone "name servers" stored in our computers. We type in a name (or click on it) and the telephone number is made available for dialing. In addition, the computer usually performs the dialing operations for us.

Source and Destination IDs

Before concluding this chapter, let's add some more information to the packet. In Figure 10.5, the packet is now expanded to include two headers. The analogy to the postal service mail is used again. Both Bob and Ted are now assigned network names and network addresses.

The most important part of this expanded example is that there are now two sets of IDs: (a) destination and source names (the originator is called the source) and (b) destination and source addresses.

The source IDs are quite important. They are used in several operations, and the one of interest here is at the destination, where they reveal the origination of the traffic. Therefore, Bob and Bob's computer can send packets back to Ted and need only reverse the addresses in the fields of the message and the packet. And this reversal is done automatically by Bob's computer.

Two names and two addresses

(a) The email (inside the envelope or packet)

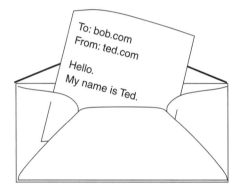

(b) Outside: the packet header

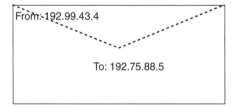

Figure 10.5 Source and Destination Addresses

The Addresses Can Vary

Keep in mind that the contents of the IP addresses will vary depending on the type of traffic in the payload. For example, if Ted were sending email (and not an instant message or an H.323 packet), the destination address would be that of a designated mail server.

Summary

The common lament of living in our modern society "Am I a number or a name?" won't get the complainer very far in a computer network. We are both, and a name server lets us take on many names if we wish.

The network name allows a user to move to different networks yet keep the same name. Of course, the network name is easier to use than an address. We also introduced another vital network component, the name server, and showed how the name server correlates the network names of Ted and Bob with their associated network addresses.

We also learned that the network name is often called an email address, and this so-called address is used with other sessions, such as chat messages and file transfers.

Chapter 11

Connecting to the Data Network

This chapter expands the explanations of how user computers are connected to networks. It also explains the role of a specific implementation of the packet switch, the *router*.

This chapter issues a temporary good-bye to the telephone (and the telephone network) with the assumption that it is indeed present, performing its functions, but transparent to its data users. This approach will allow us to examine the behavior of data networks without worrying about the telephone connection. In essence, it is there, and we don't care—just as long as it stays there.

Revisiting the Switch

In earlier chapters, we saw that the email or chat message from Ted to Bob is sent to Ted's local Central Office (telephone office) where it is relayed by switches to Bob or Bob's server. This idea is shown again in Figure 11.1.

We also learned that the switch is programmed to know the best route to reach Bob. All the switches in the network are programmed to support this Ted-to-Bob session. I also promised that we would see how the switch can be so smart to perform these services. The next four chapters are devoted to this explanation.

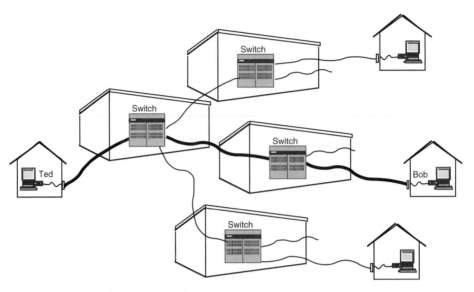

Figure 11.1   Switching, Examined Again

Through the Telephone Local Exchange to the Data Network

The discussions thus far have been about transmitting Ted's packets to Bob through the telephone network. But the path between Ted and Bob most likely is through the sending and receiving telephone exchanges, shown in Figure 11.2, and a separate nontelephone network. The most prominent names are *data network* and *packet network*, and several references have been made to these terms in previous chapters. They are so named because this type of network transports data traffic in the form of packets (such as email) and not voice traffic (such as a telephone conversation).[1]

In most situations, the transmission of the email from Ted to Bob entails the use of the telephone links (the local loop) to get the message from Ted's

---

1. An exception is an emerging technology called voice over IP (VoIP). This procedure carries the digital voice speech in a packet, just like data. See a related book in this series (*Voice Over IP*) for more information.

Figure 11.2   Connecting to the Data (Packet) Network

PC to the telephone Central Office (CO). But from the CO, the email takes a different path.

At the CO, another device diverts Ted's data message to the data network. This device may be a switch, or it may be a very simple device, such as a "panel" that cross-connects Ted's local loop wires (from his home) to another set of wires to this other packet network. (These details are not important for this discussion, so they are not shown in the figure.) If analog links are being used between the customer and the telephone exchanges, modems are required, as described in Chapter 4.

As noted, the data network is not designed for any other traffic but data. It does not give very good service to voice conversations because it usually holds packets (containing either voice or data) in memory (a queue) to make decisions about how to process the packet. This delay for voice packets can be quite annoying to two persons engaged in a conversation, because variable delays can occur in delivering the traffic to each listener. These ideas are explained in Chapter 7.

Why Use the Telephone Exchange?

You might be thinking: Why bother sending Ted's email through the telephone system in the first place? Why not just send it directly to the data network? As suggested in Figure 11.3, the approach seems inefficient.

At first glance, it appears that this approach is adding unnecessary steps. But the steps are necessary; there is no other alternative, at least for now.

This seems inefficient:

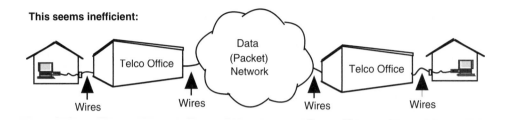

Why not this arrangement?

Figure 11.3 Why Use the Telephone Network for Data?

Recall that Ted's message must have a medium (a wire or a wireless path) on which to "ride" over to Bob's computer.

The only wires out of most residences and businesses are the telephone company's wires. Those wires go to the telephone office. Consequently, it is necessary to use the telephone system. That is the reason for using the modem. It allows the transport of the digital, binary 1s and 0s over the telephone's analog links.

So the answer to the question, why use the telephone system for transporting data is answered by posing two more questions with their answers:

    ❏ Where do those wires from the house go?
       Answer: To the telephone office

    ❏ Who owns them?
       Answer: The telephone company

Why Not Use the Cable TV Network?

Some Internet users opt for using the cable TV network to get their traffic to and from the Internet. Indeed, cable modems are becoming quite popular. You may wish to refer to Chapter 6 for a review of this issue.

Hereafter, Assume the Existence of the Telco or Cable TV Links

Even though the modem and the telephone system or cable TV links are absolutely essential for an end-to-end connection between computers, we can ignore them with the knowledge that these components allow Ted and Bob to send and receive packets of data between their two computers and their servers, as shown in Figure 11.4. Of course, the links are still there, but as long as they are doing their job, we need not be concerned with them.

We salute the modem and the telephone/cable TV networks for their fine services, but hereafter concentrate (with a few exceptions in subsequent chapters) on data networks (and soon the Internet), as shown in Figure 11.4.

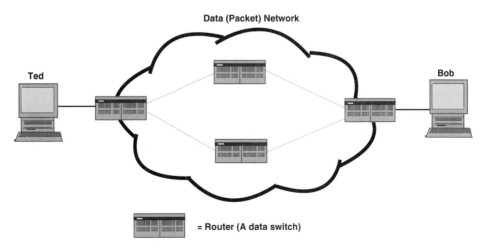

Figure 11.4   The Data Network and the Router

The Packet Switch is a Router

Another piece is now added to the Networking 101 puzzle. It is called a *router*. This machine performs the same functions as the packet switch, introduced earlier. Indeed, it is really nothing more than an example of a packet switch.

Its job is to relay packets through the data (packet) network. It is different from the switch at the telephone offices in that it is designed for data traffic. It can certainly handle voice traffic, but that is not what it is intended to do. Likewise, the telephone switch can handle data traffic, but that is not what it is intended to do.

A frequently asked question is: Why is the router not called a packet switch if they do the same thing? The answer is that these terms were coined by their inventors. I don't mean they just made up terms; it is just that they had to name their invention something. Both terms convey the concept of relaying and forwarding of data traffic, so they are aptly named.

One way to view the terms packet switch and router is that a router is a specific implementation of a packet switch. Many people use the terms interchangeably.

Also, keep in mind that the users' traffic may also be sent to other machines in the data network. For example, if the user traffic is email, the packets are sent to an email server (see scenario 4 in Appendix A).

Summary

The transmission of the data packets from Ted to Bob entails the use of the telephone and of the telephone links (the local loop) to get the message from Ted's PC to the telephone Central Office (CO). But from the CO, the email takes a different path, usually through a data network (and routers and servers), one that is designed to handle data.

Until residences and office buildings have connections (wires, cables, antenna) that allow data traffic to bypass the telephone and cable TV systems, the present arrangement will continue. But to understand further details about data and computer networking, we can just assume the basic telephone or cable TV services are in place and working.

Chapter **12**

Routing Traffic Through the Network

This chapter looks inside the network cloud and examines the operations to route Ted's packets to the destination user, Bob, in Chicago. The subject of routing tables is explained, as are the actions of the routers with regard to these routing tables and the processing of the packet.

Once again, it will be helpful to use the postal service as an analogy to the network routing operations. In addition, we add another analogy to the discussion, with a comparison of the routing tables in the network to a road map.

Comparing Postal Bins and Router Queues

In the example of the post office, personnel or sorters are tasked with examining the "To" address on the envelope to decide how to send the mail to the recipient. For a manual post office, the mail clerk reads the destination address and places the envelope in a designated bin. This bin serves as a queue for the letters that are going to that destination. Figure 12.1 shows this process.

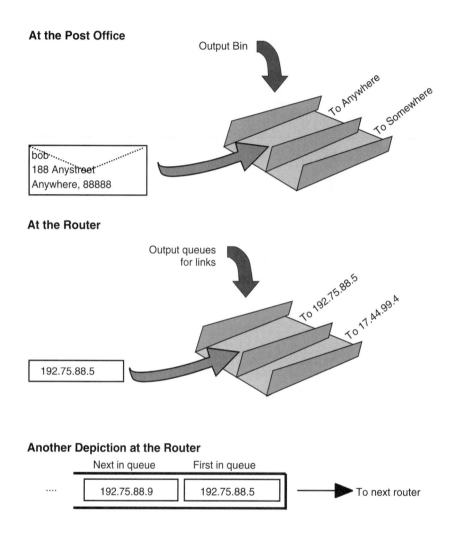

Figure 12.1 Routing the Letter and the Packet

It is easy to see the analogy of the postal clerk to the router, and the output bin to the router's output link. The router also has "output bins," but they are called output queues. They consist of computer memory and they store the packets awaiting transmission onto the communications link.

The queues often contain multiple packets, as shown in the bottom part of Figure 12.1. They are placed in a queue and usually taken out of the queue and sent onto the link to the next router or the final destination, based on when they arrived at the queue. It is usually a first-come, first-served basis, much like we do when we queue up in a line at the bank or the movie theater.

Revisiting the Locations of Ted and Bob in the Network

Figure 12.2 revisits the view of the computer network, with the addition of more routers. It shows the locations of our two users and their computers, Ted in San Diego and Bob in Chicago. Don't forget that they are connected through the telephone local loops, then through the telephone switches (or some type of connector at the Central Office), to a router. At this router the email enters the data network, and the packets are routed to the receiving computer or the computer's server.

The actual route of the packets from San Diego to Chicago can vary. Figure 12.2 illustrates that the packets could go through a San Francisco router, a Dallas router, a Denver router, and so on. These router locations are called *nodes*. Under certain situations, the traffic may even go through some of the other nodes, such as Atlanta. These situations are explored later in this chapter.

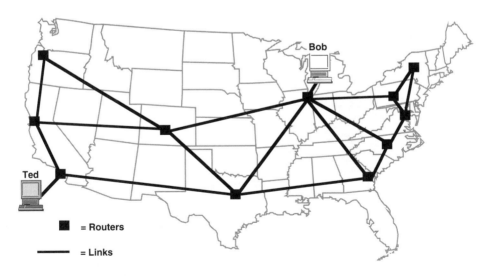

Figure 12.2   Connecting the Computers with Routers and Links

Using Destination Addresses to Make Routing Decisions

To learn how the user packets are routed through the data network, we need to revisit the subject of addresses. Figure 12.3 shows that the two computers are identified with these addresses: 192.75.88.5 for Bob's computer, and 192.99.43.4 for Ted's computer.

Figure 12.3 also shows that the packets can be sent to one or more routers (for this example, the routers at San Diego, Dallas, and Chicago). The routers use the destination address in the packet header of the incoming packet to determine how the packets are routed; that is, to which output link the packet is to be sent in order to reach Bob's computer.

The other links and routers in the network are available to support the packet's journey through the network, and some of them will be brought into play later.

The packet header is filled in at the sending computer to contain both the source and destination addresses, in the same way an envelope is made up for

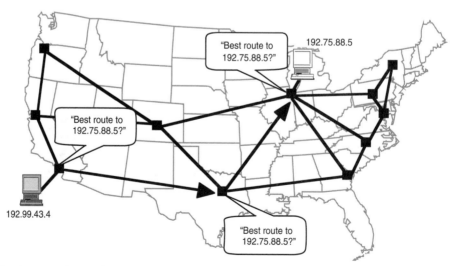

Figure 12.3   Using the Destination Address to Determine the Route

the postal service. Like the post office, each router examines the destination address in the header to determine how to route the packet to the final destination, Bob's computer.

Addresses for the Routers

Each router node in the network has an address, just as each post office has an address. For this analysis, it is necessary to assign addresses to the routers that will be involved in the transport of the user traffic or that may be selected as a backup in case the first choice router link is not available (because of link or router failures). These router addresses are shown in Figure 12.4 and are assigned as follows:

San Francisco:	192.88.88.88
Dallas:	192.99.99.99
Atlanta:	192.77.77.77
Chicago:	192.66.66.66

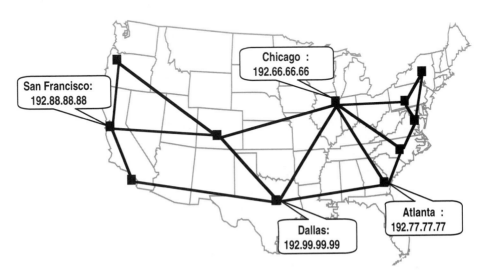

Figure 12.4   Addresses of the Routers

The Routing Table[1]

The ability of the router to decide how to route a packet to a destination address is similar to the ability of the postal clerk to decide the proper slot in the mail bin in which to place a letter for its journey to its recipient. The postal clerk has learned that a specific bin slot is the correct slot to use to send a letter to its destination. Likewise, the router has also learned about the correct queue for an outgoing link to send a packet to its destination.

For the postal clerk, the knowledge could be "stored" in the clerk's mind or the clerk might look at a printed list that provides guidance on which bin is appropriate for a destination address.

For the router, this knowledge is stored in its memory in the *routing table*. An abbreviated routing table is shown in Figure 12.5. It contains several entries, three of which are shown: (a) the destination address, (b) the address of the next node that is to receive the packet (the primary route), and (c) the address of an alternate node (the secondary route) that will receive the packet in the event that problems occur on the primary route.

Comparing the routing table to a road map is a useful exercise. After all, the routing table shows the topology of the network, just like a road map shows the topology of a highway road system. The routing table also shows how to get from one part of the network to another, and that is what a road map does as well.

Sending the Packet to Dallas and Processing It

The same payload is being used in these examples as was used in earlier explanations: "Hello. My name is Ted." As you may recall, this payload has been divided into two packets, each with a header containing a destination address. The first packet only is shown in these examples and in Figure 12.6. Based on the forwarding decisions made at the San Diego router, the packet is sent to the next node router, located in Dallas.

---

1. In some recent literature the routing table is called a forwarding table.

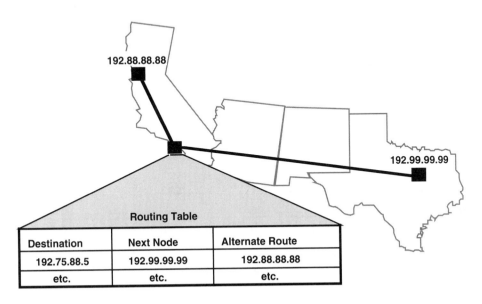

Figure 12.5 The Routing Table at San Diego

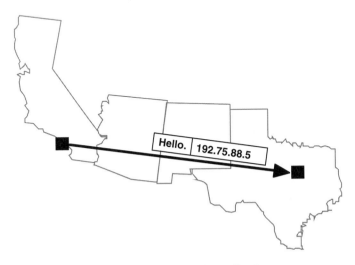

Figure 12.6 The Packet Is Sent to the Dallas Router

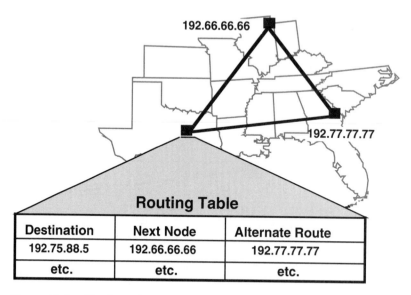

Figure 12.7   Checking the Dallas Routing Table

Processing the Packet at the Dallas Router

Upon the packet arriving at the Dallas router (see Figure 12.7), the destination address in the packet is checked against the destination addressees in the router's routing table. If a match is found, an entry of the table contains information about the next node that is to receive the packet. In this example, it is the address of the Chicago router. As before, the table also contains an entry of the address of an alternate route, Atlanta in this case.

Sending the Packet to the Chicago Router and Processing It

The forwarding operation is repeated at each router, and as Figure 12.8 shows, the packet is sent out of the Dallas router's output link to the Chicago node.

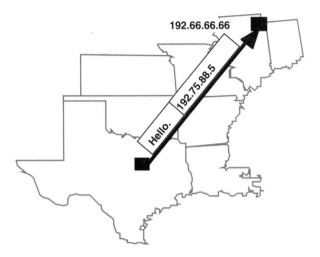

Figure 12.8   Sending the Packet to the Chicago Node

Processing the Packet at the Chicago Router

In Figure 12.9, the packet arrives at the Chicago router that directly supports (connects to) the destination host machine (Bob's PC). The router knows that the packet need not be forwarded to any other router because the routing table entry for the address of Bob's PC signifies that address 172.75.88.5 is "directly attached" to this router. This term means there are no intervening nodes between the router and the destination machine. So, the packet is delivered to Bob's computer, through the intervening telephone office, and local loop.

Dealing With a Mail Server if a Mail Server Is Involved

If the traffic is conventional email, it is not sent directly to Bob, as shown in Figure 12.8. Rather, the packets are sent to Bob's email server. Moreover, the destination IP address in the packet header would be the address of the mail server. Later, Bob logs on to the network and to his mail server. After that, Ted's email message is sent by Bob's server to Bob's PC.

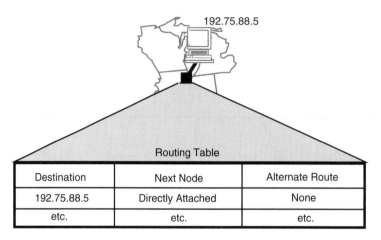

Routing Table		
Destination	Next Node	Alternate Route
192.75.88.5	Directly Attached	None
etc.	etc.	etc.

Figure 12.9 The Packet Is Processed by the Chicago Router

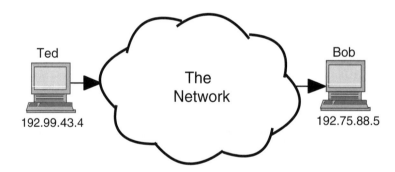

Figure 12.10 From the View of the Network Cloud

Routing Activities from the Users' View

Earlier in this book, the idea of the network cloud was introduced. It is shown once again in Figure 12.10. From the end users' perspective (Ted and Bob), all they really care about is that they can exchange their email. Most people would rather not see all the details we have unearthed in this chapter. But of course, this population does not include you. After all, you are reading the *Networking 101* book!

Summary

In this chapter, the network was examined in relation to the operations of the router nodes. Routing tables were introduced and a comparison was made of these tables to road maps. Using another analogy, the queues in the routers are similar to the outgoing postal bins in the postal system; they are used to hold the packets until they can be sent to the next node in the network.

Chapter 13

Backup and
Route Discovery

This chapter expands on the previous chapter's explanations of how networks route traffic. Additionally, we examine how the routes are discovered through address advertising and how the routing tables are built. Another important discussion in this chapter is how networks can ensure the safe delivery of customers' packets through alternate routes by using backup links and routers.

Using Alternate Routes for Backup Operations

Alternate route entries in the routing table provide just that: alternate routes. In Figure 13.1, the link between Dallas and Chicago is out of service. This situation may occur for a number of reasons, perhaps a backhoe digging up the wires running between Dallas and Chicago or a faulty interface at one of the routers. Or the link may be taken out of service by network management for maintenance.

Alternate routes are quite important to the network provider. After all, if the provider does not deliver the payload between paying customers, the provider will not get paid. An inoperable link or a failed router results in undeliverable payload and is not an acceptable situation to the service provider.

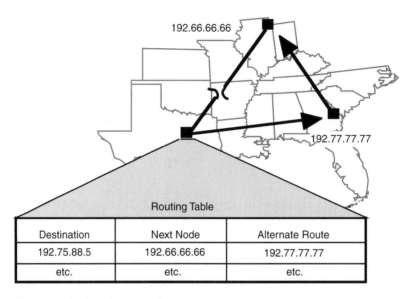

Routing Table		
Destination	Next Node	Alternate Route
192.75.88.5	192.66.66.66	192.77.77.77
etc.	etc.	etc.

Figure 13.1 The Alternate Route

Nor is it acceptable to the users of the network. If they continue to experience a loss of service, such as undelivered user traffic, from the standpoint of the network provider, Ted and Bob will become virtual customers.

Consequences of Network Failures

Network failures can have serious consequences, most of which result in lost revenue and lost productivity. For example, failures to parts of the U.S. telephone network during the past few years (and the failures are rare, to give credit to the telephone network providers) have resulted in millions of dollars lost to the network's customers. Not to mention the psychological toll a failure takes during family emergencies, and so on.

In many networks, the motto is "Whatever it takes, whatever it costs, keep the network up." With this thought in mind, in Figure 13.1, it can be seen from the routing table and from the topology of the network that an alternate path is available through the Atlanta node to Chicago and the destination user, Bob, or Bob's server.

Discovering Problems

How does the Dallas router know that it cannot use the link to Chicago? Earlier discussions introduced the concept of an acknowledgment, an ACK. With this simple operation, it is an easy matter to know about the failure. Figure 13.2 is used for this discussion.

It works this way. First, upon Dallas sending a packet to Chicago, the Dallas router starts a timer. Second, the Dallas node keeps a copy (in a queue) of the packet it sent to Chicago.

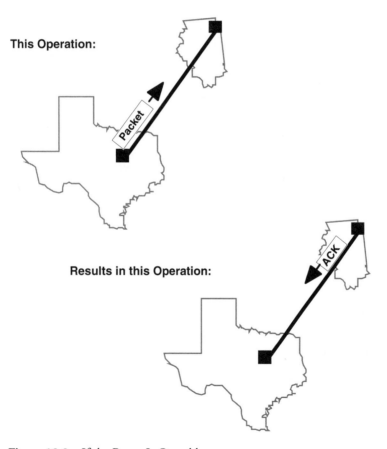

This Operation:

Results in this Operation:

Figure 13.2 If the Route Is Operable

The Route Is Operable

The timer keeps running until one of two events occurs. If the Chicago node receives the packet, it must send back to Dallas a packet that contains an ACK. Upon receiving this ACK packet, Dallas knows the transmitted packet has arrived safely at Chicago and it can turn off the timer. Dallas can also delete the copy of the packet it was saving in its queue, since the packet is now at Chicago and is the responsibility of the Chicago router.

This same type of operation occurs between all nodes in this network that process this packet, first between San Diego and Dallas, then from Dallas to Chicago. So, the packet is relayed from node to node, something like passing a baton in a relay race.

This operation repeats itself until the packet is delivered to the final destination. If the packet recipient is in the far reaches of the planet, it makes no difference. If the users can log on to the Internet, they can communicate with each other.

The Route Is Not Operable

The second possibility is that the packet does not arrive at the Chicago router because of a failure. This situation is shown in Figure 13.3.

The timer at the Dallas router expires, because the Dallas router has not received the ACK. With the timer expired, the Dallas router (perhaps after making a few attempts to resend the packet on the Chicago link) consults the routing table to find an alternate link. In this example, the table reveals that an alternate link is available to Chicago through Atlanta.

The same sequence of events now takes place between Dallas and Atlanta. Dallas retrieves the packet from the queue, sends the packet to Atlanta, starts the timer again, and still keeps a copy of the packet.

When an ACK is received from Atlanta, Dallas knows that the packet has been relayed successfully to the next node. Dallas can delete its copy of the packet.

The Atlanta router repeats this process to relay the packet to Chicago, the final router in the path to Bob's machine or his server.

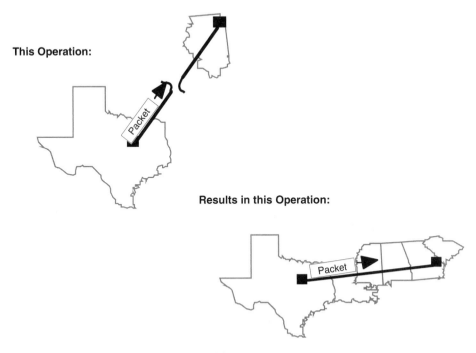

Figure 13.3 If the Route Is Not Operable

Acknowledgment Operations May Not Happen

All these ACKs of Ted and Bob's payload might not occur. It depends on the design of the network. If the network is operating at very high speeds, the routers are sending and receiving so many packets a second that they have neither the time nor the resources to send an ACK for their received traffic.

This situation can occur if the links between the routers are high bandwidth optical fibers. In this situation, the router periodically sends a control packet to its neighbors (a Hello packet) just to make sure they are up and running.

What happens to the ACKs for the end-user payload? After all, acknowledging the Hello packet is not the same as acknowledging Ted's packet.

If user traffic is lost or damaged, Ted and Bob want to make sure it is recovered. It may surprise you to know that in any systems, namely, the PC you may have in front of you, these ACKs are sent from the users' machines.

135

What a great idea. The network no longer has to keep track of the traffic anymore; the responsibility is now at the user computer. Of course, Ted and Bob don't know there is a software program (a protocol) inside their machines that is holding a copy of the packet in its queue, sending the packet, starting a timer, and awaiting a reply—just like the routers did in this example. You may have heard of this protocol; it is called TCP, for the Transmission Control Protocol.

Once again, if the traffic is being sent to a server (a Web server, an email server), these ACKs and NAKs take place between user machines and the servers.

Building the Road Map with Route Advertising

How do these routers know so much? How can they know about the best route to reach Bob? They know because a special control protocol is executed in the routers to advertise (a) Bob's address and (b) the path (also called the route) through the network that can be taken for a packet to reach Bob or Bob's server.

These advertisements are placed in special control packets by the advertising machine and sent to the machine's "neighbor" nodes; that is, the nodes that are directly connected to the advertising node by a communications link. In turn, these nodes then send the advertisement packets to their neighbors. Eventually, all interested nodes find out about (say) Bob's address.

If the nodes are not interested, they ignore the advertisement, or in many situations, they will not receive the advertisement because of policies established by network managers. (You do not have the phone numbers in your directory of everyone in the world, because the telephone companies have agreements about how the phone numbers are advertised and disseminated.)

In Figure 13.4, the Chicago router is advertising Bob's address to Dallas and Atlanta. For ease of reference, I am not showing addresses, but names; don't forget that addresses are advertised. The key contents in the packets are (a) Bob's address, (b) the address of the advertising node (the Chicago router), and (c) the number of hops to the advertised address from the advertising node. Hop simply means how many nodes are between Ted and the advertising machine.

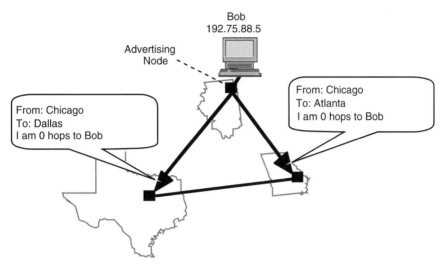

Figure 13.4   From Chicago to Dallas About Bob's Address (Note: This example shows names for simplicity, but addresses are being advertised)

The advertisement from Chicago states "0 hops" because the Chicago router is connected directly to Bob's machine or a server.[1]

Atlanta Relays the Advertisement

Next, Atlanta relays this advertisement packet to Dallas, as shown in Figure 13.5.

Before sending the packet, the Atlanta node changes these fields. It places its address in the "advertising address" field, and it adds the value of 1 to the hop field. In effect, the Atlanta router states, "Hello Dallas, this is Atlanta. I want you to know that Bob can be reached through me, and I am one hop away from Bob."

---

1. Hop count is one way of advertising. Others are how much bandwidth (capacity) is available, how secure the link is, how reliable it is, and so on.

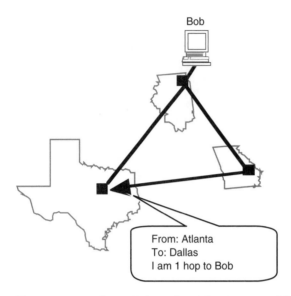

Figure 13.5 Atlanta Relays the Advertisement (Note: This example shows names for simplicity, but addresses are being advertised)

Although not shown in Figure 13.5, the Dallas router sends back an ACK packet to Atlanta which means, "Thanks. I will remember this information, and I now know that I can reach Bob going though Atlanta. My hop count to Bob is 2, since yours is 1."

The Dallas router stores this information in its routing table for later use. Subsequently, when it receives a packet with the destination address for Bob in it, the router knows how many hops it takes to reach Bob through Atlanta, as well as through Chicago.

Result of the Advertisements at Dallas

The result of the address advertisements is that the Dallas router knows how to reach Bob's address. Even better, it knows of two routes to reach Bob: (a) through Chicago and (b) through Atlanta, as depicted in Figure 13.6.

When the Dallas router receives a packet, say, from San Diego and destined for Bob's address, its routing table reveals that the route through Chicago (and

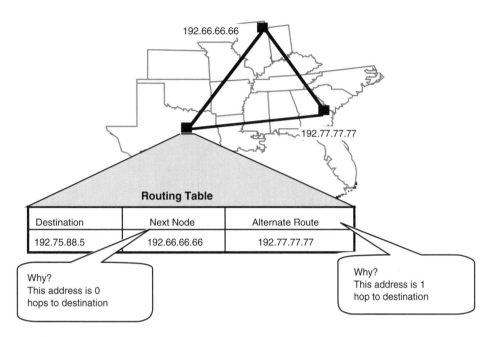

Figure 13.6   Advertising Is Reflected in Routing Tables

not Atlanta) is preferable. Why? Because the Dallas-to-Chicago route has fewer hops than the Dallas-to-Atlanta route.

Choosing a route based on the fewest number of hops is usually the preferred approach because it often translates into less delay. After all, each node in the path consumes time to process a packet. Furthermore, it is also desirable to have as few machines as possible processing the payload because each processing machine introduces additional costs and overhead to support Ted and Bob's chat session.[2]

I am reminded of a bureaucracy where employees read memos about which they have no concern. They waste a lot of time processing this superfluous correspondence. It is the same situation with the router, and unlike the idle

2. The fewest-number-of-hops approach to routing traffic can present problems. It may lead to parts of the network being underused. Therefore, many networks have a means to divert traffic to parts of the network that may be underused, something like our moving to a shorter queue at the registers of a grocery store. This idea is called constrained routing.

bureaucrat, the router is likely busy processing other packets. I am also reminded of the efficient and busy bureaucrat who places a sign on his/her desk, "It has come to the attention of this desk that too much is coming to this desk."

The data network is designed in the same manner: don't send packets to a node unless it is essential. To do otherwise can have unfortunate consequences. After all, high-speed computers such as routers can generate hundreds of thousands of packets per second. Even a small fraction of those packets, if not needed, can degrade the performance of a network significantly. In effect, a network node should say, "It has come to the attention of this node that too much is coming to this node."

Summary

"Whatever it takes, keep the network up and running" is the credo of many network managers and their organizations. And with good reason, for network failures can have serious consequences.

For modern voice and data networks, the use of backup routes provides a means to recover from link and node failures. This vital service uses the concepts of route advertising and route discovery. Of course, the operations not only build a "road map" in the routing tables for backup purposes, but the operations also provide for efficient routing.

Chapter 14

The Internet and Internet Service Providers (ISPs)

We have referred to the Internet several times in this book. Recall that I explained it would be helpful in reading this book if you had previously logged on to the Internet.

In this chapter, we finally introduce the Internet in a more formal way, and what you will discover in this chapter I think will please you. In earlier chapters, we have been laying the groundwork for this chapter. Consequently, you know many of the features of the Internet. Our approach in this chapter is to put a few more pieces into the Networking 101 puzzle and to step back and take a look at the part of the puzzle completed so far.

Finally and Formally Introducing the Internet

The Internet was developed to support the transfer of data traffic (packets) between computers, workstations, and other machines. The Internet owes its origin to some pioneering endeavors performed at the U.S. Department of

141

Defense (DOD) in the mid-1960s. At that time, the DOD's Advanced Research Projects Agency (ARPA) was tasked with doling out research dollars and coordinating research projects within the DOD.

During that time, ARPA was a great benefactor to researchers. The U.S. government provided an extensive budget for research and often was in charge of coordinating and providing funds for the various projects. One of the big projects focused on packet networks, a technology that was in its infancy at that time. Much of ARPA's work led to many of the ideas and concepts explained in this book and, of course, to the Internet.

The term *internet* is used in two separate contexts. If the word has an uppercase I, it refers to the public Internet that is used commercially. In contrast, if the word begins with a lowercase i, it refers to a set of networks that do not belong to the public Internet. These internets are usually privately owned. Another term that is used to describe a private internet is an *intranet*.

The Internet is shown in Figure 14.1 with the network cloud. This depiction is quite useful, for it would be an impossible task to show in one picture all the computers, routers and links that make up the Internet. There are thousands of them.

Let's see what we have learned. The list below describes several of the major features of the Internet. Take a look at the list; the topics should be familiar. If they are not, I have noted the chapter or appendix where these topics can be reviewed.

- ❐ Many connections to the Internet are analog and need modems (Chapter 4).
- ❐ The Internet is a digital network (Chapter 5).
- ❐ The Internet is a data network (Chapter 7).
- ❐ The Internet multiplexes user traffic (Chapter 8).
- ❐ The Internet is a packet network (Chapter 8).
- ❐ The Internet uses IP addresses for traffic forwarding (Chapter 9).
- ❐ The Internet uses network names for ease of reference (Chapter 10).
- ❐ The Internet forwards packets with routing tables (Chapter 12).

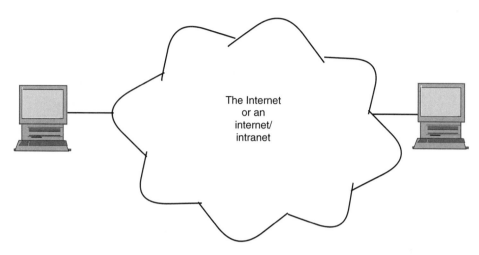

Figure 14.1   The Internet (or internet)

❏ The Internet can recover from failures (Chapter 13).

❏ The Internet advertises addresses to discover routes anywhere in the world (Chapter 13).

❏ Different methods are available for exchanging information through the Internet (Appendix A).

The network cloud in Figure 14.1 should not look so mysterious anymore. But I also recognize that we are covering a lot of territory in this book. So, you may want to pause here and review some of these topics if they are still a bit vague.

Connecting to the Internet

Most individuals' hosts do not connect directly into the Internet cloud. Rather, a user computer is first connected to an access node (such as a router or a machine called a *dial-in server* or a *remote access server*), usually through a conventional telephone dial-up operation. The access system can take several forms. It can be a node sponsored by a government agency, a university, a research center, or a commercial company, such as AOL.

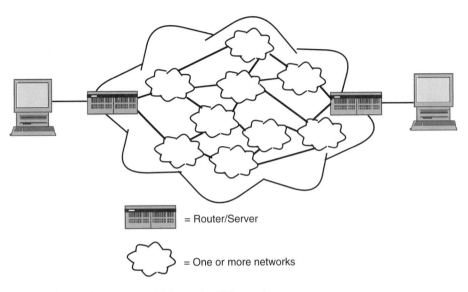

= Router/Server

= One or more networks

Figure 14.2   The Internet: A Network of Networks

Most of the discussions in this book have focused on routers. Often, a remote access server is used to handle some of the procedures for getting connected to the Internet. Figure 14.2 reflects this idea. Although a server and a router can be different machines, one machine can perform both functions. The reason I bring up the topic of a remote access server is that this term is often mentioned in user manuals and ISP customer literature. But it is not essential to our understanding of the Internet architecture.

Supporting Millions of Computers and Thousands of Networks

Figure 14.2 also shows that the Internet is a complex conglomeration of thousands of networks, connected by routers and communications links.

You may be inclined to wonder how these thousands of networks, routers, hosts, and servers can communicate with each other. Well, you should not be so inclined! Our examples in previous chapters demonstrated that the use of address advertising and routing tables allows anyone on earth (who can dial in to the Internet) to communicate with anyone who is also on the Net.

All that is needed to achieve this remarkable feat is (a) a PC, (b) a dial-up modem, and (c) access to an ISP. In Chapters 12 and 13, we learned how Ted's and Bob's packets can be exchanged between San Diego and Chicago, through Dallas, and perhaps Atlanta. Figure 14.2 is nothing more than an expansion of these concepts. What is happening inside those network clouds is the same as what happened in our email users' network cloud.

Don't be intimidated by the size of the Internet. Our discussions have explained a microcosm of its basic operations. We need a few more pieces to the Networking 101 puzzle to complete our view, and these pieces will be placed into the puzzle in the remaining chapters.

The Internet Service Providers (ISPs)

Many service providers for Internet access are competitive companies and price their services based on what they provide to a user. By necessity, these service providers were mentioned in earlier parts of this book. They are called ISPs, for *Internet Service Providers*.

Many ISPs are available, especially in large metropolitan areas. Most of them provide similar services, such as support of email applications and accesses to other sites to obtain information (stock quotes, news, and so on). Figure 14.3 shows two examples of ISPs, AOL and IBM. One ISP supports Ted's connection, and another (or the same) supports Bob's connection. In turn, these two ISPs connect to each other.

How the ISPs Connect To Each Other

The ISPs connect to each other by one of two arrangements. The first arrangement is called *peering*. The two ISPs agree to connect directly to each other without transiting another ISP. This arrangement means the two ISPs have routers that are connected directly with communications links, such as optical fiber cables. Typically, peering ISPs do not charge each other for exchanging traffic but assume a shared cost model. The two peers do not bother about settlement costs and revenue.

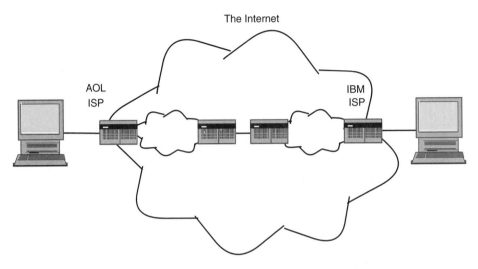

Figure 14.3 Internet Service Providers (ISPs)

The second arrangement is called *transiting*. The two ISPs connect to each other through a third-party network. Typically, the transit network charges the ISPs for its services to them.

The decision of an ISP to enter into a peering or transit arrangement with another service provider is usually transparent to Ted and Bob.

Summary

The Internet is an example and an implementation of many of the Networking 101 operations we have learned in this book. The checklist in this chapter revealed that you now know a lot about data networks and the Internet. But a few more pieces have yet to be placed in the puzzle. They are explained in the following chapters.

Chapter 15

Network IDs: Domain Names

Network names have been described several times in this book, and Chapter 10 was devoted to explaining their functions. In this chapter we pick up where we left off in Chapter 10 and focus on a remarkable but simple Internet name server system. It is called the *Domain Name System* (DNS), and it is a vital piece of the Networking 101 puzzle. Indeed, the Internet as it is used today (as well as the Web, explained in Chapter 18) could not exist without DNS.

Review of Network Names

In Chapter 10, we learned that a name is not an address and therefore does not have any location significance, such as a data network ID or a telephone area code. I emphasized that names are intended to have no location significance. Part of their intent is to be independent of any geographical constraint. I also emphasized that a user-friendly name is easier to use than a cumbersome IP address. Chapter 10 introduced the name server, whose job is to correlate nonroutable names with routable addresses.

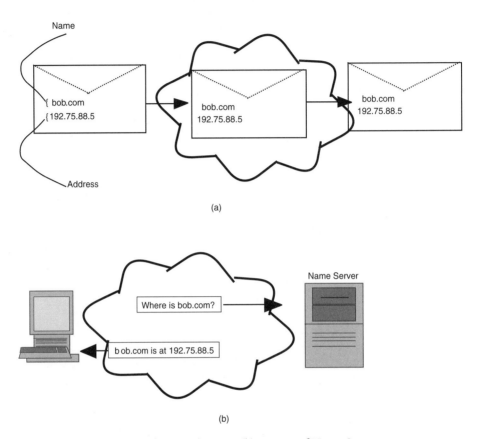

Figure 15.1 (a) Review of Network Name (b) Review of Name Server

Figure 15.1, presented in Chapter 10, is shown once again in a more general way to serve as a review of the concepts of a network name and a name server.

Hierarchical Names

Like the IP addresses, names can have hierarchical significance, an idea shown in Figure 15.2. For example, the network name (registered in the Internet) for my company, Information Engineering Institute, is infoinst. Certainly infoinst has no hierarchical aspect; it's just a flat name.

But consider these names: (a) rd.infoinst.com and (b) sales.infoinst.com. Each of the dots in the name signifies levels of hierarchy. The top part of the

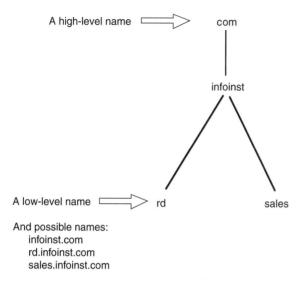

Figure 15.2   Hierarchical Names

hierarchy is com, the next level is infoinst, and the bottom levels are rd (for research and development) and sales.

The hierarchical idea is valuable when storing and retrieving names in a directory. For example, we might wish to access information on infoinst.com in general. Therefore, the name infoinst.com would include information also from the lower names in the name domain of R&D and sales.

The idea is also valuable for identifying an organization in the Internet. Let's say that I only want to make infoinst.com known to the outside world. Therefore, I do not publish in a directory (a public directory, something like a telephone directory) the rd and the sales parts of my company's name. They remain private to Information Engineering Institute.

A naming hierarchy is also called a naming (or name) *domain*. The term domain refers to all names that are associated with a name. This idea is another way of saying a name domain refers to a name space. In this example, the high-level name domain is com, and the next level domain is infoinst.com, and so forth. The complete name space (domain) is any name under com in the hierarchy.

Name Domains and Name Servers

Name servers are associated with the name domain. In Figure 15.3, a *root* name server is at the top of the naming domain. Its main job is to direct name-to-address queries to an *authoritative* name server. The authoritative name server is so called because it has complete information about that part of the domain name space for which is it responsible. It is responsible for the accuracy of the name and address IDs in the name server.

For example, the root server typically would not have the information about rd.infoinst.com. Rather, it would have information about the authoritative name server that is storing this information.

The top-level authoritative name server can delegate portions of the infoinst.com namespace to departmental name servers, such as rd and sales. Thus, a department within Information Engineering gains a measure of autonomy in creating and managing the names within its *subdomain*. For example, the subdomains of rd.infoinst.com and sales.infoinst.com can be served by other name servers.

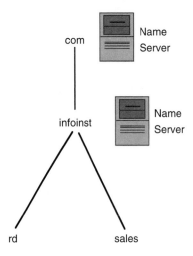

Figure 15.3 The Name Servers

The Domain Name System (DNS)

The Internet has a valuable naming/addressing architecture called the *Domain Name System* (DNS). DNS is a worldwide directory for Internet names and their associated addresses. It is similar to the worldwide telephone directory wherein a name is associated with a telephone number.

The concept of the DNS is shown in Figure 15.4, which is a portion of the DNS.

DNS is organized around a *root* and *tree* structure. A root has no higher entry and is also called a parent to the lower levels of the tree. The tree consists of *branches* that connect *nodes*; the nodes have names called *labels*.

The label must be a relative distinguished name—distinguishable relative to this node level. This idea is quite simple: make sure the domain names are always unique. For example, infoinst.com exists only once under the root of com, but it can exist again under, say, org.

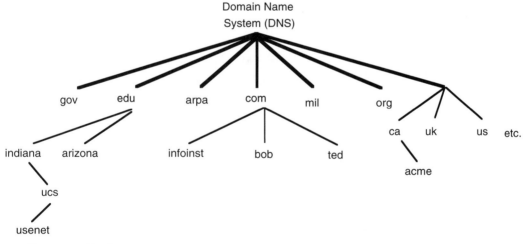

gov: Government body
edu: Educational institution
arpa: ARPANET-Internet host
com: Commercial enterprise
mil: Military organizations
org: Any other organization
ca, etc.: ISO standard for names of countries (ISO 3166)

Figure 15.4   The Domain Name System (DNS; registration examples, some hypothetical)

The hierarchical naming is established by tracing down through the tree, selecting the names attached to each label, and concatenating these labels to form a distinguished name—distinguishable at all levels in the tree.

Notice that infoinst is registered under com (actual registration), and so are Bob and Ted (examples only). Indiana University and the University of Arizona are registered under edu (actual registrations). Acme is registered under ca (Canada) (an example).

The Internet DNS Root Servers

Table 15-1 shows the locations and sponsoring organizations of the Internet DNS root servers. Most of them are sponsored by government agencies, colleges/universities, and nonprofit organizations. Some are operated by private companies. The Web sites listed in the table provide information on each of these DNS sponsors. You can also find many papers and tutorials on DNS at these sites.

Using DNS to Look Up an Address

When Ted enters bob.com (again, a hypothetical example), say, to look at Bob's Web site, the following events occur:

1. Ted's PC checks the name of bob.com in its internal storage (a local mapping). If it is not found,

2. unbeknown to Ted, his PC sends a query packet to a local DNS server (for example, at Ted's ISP). If not found,

3. the local DNS server sends a query packet to a designated root server.

4. The root server supplies the local DNS server with the authoritative name server for the name. The authoritative name server is queried and

5. returns address 192.75.88.5 for bob.com's Web page to the local DNS server.

6. The local DNS server returns the information to the PC.

Table 15.1   Examples of DNS Root Servers

A	Network Solutions, Inc	Herndon, VA USA	http://www.netsol.com
B	Information Sciences Institute, USC	Marina Del Rey, CA USA	http://www.isi.edu
C	PSINet	Herndon, VA USA	http://www.psi.net
D	University of Maryland	College Park, MD USA	http://www.umd.edu
E	NASA	Mountain View, CA USA	http://www.nasa.gov
F	Internet Software Consortium	Palo Alto, CA USA	http://www.isc.org
G	Defense Information Systems Agency	Vienna, VA USA	http://www.nic.mil
H	Army Research Laboratory	Aberdeen, MD USA	http://www.army.mil
I	NORDUNet	Stockholm, Sweden	http://www.nordu.net
J	To Be Determined	Herndon, VA USA	(not yet established)
K	RIPE-NCC	London, UK	http://www.ripe.net
L	IANA	Marina Del Rey, CA USA	http://www.iana.org
M	WIDE	Tokyo, Japan	http://www.wide.ad.jp

7. The PC places the address of 192.75.88.5 into the destination address of the packet header and sends the packet to its ISP. The PC also stores the record of "bob.com is at 192.75.88.5" in its internal storage for later use.

Summary

This chapter introduced the Domain Name System (DNS) and explained why DNS is an important piece of the Networking 101 puzzle. The Internet and internets would be very difficult to use if DNS did not exist. We also examined the DNS servers and looked at examples of several DNS root servers. The chapter concluded with a description of what happens when Ted enters Bob's DNS name into his PC in order to send traffic to Bob's Web page.

Chapter 16

Putting It Together

If you have been following our analysis of networks thus far, you should find this chapter a simple review. There is no new material here, just an explanation that puts the pieces of the puzzle into the larger context of the overall Networking 101 puzzle.

Eight events are described, from the moment Ted enters Bob's message into his computer, to the transmission of this packet into the network, to the arrival of the packet at Bob's computer.

Obtaining Bob's Address

In Figure 16.1, Ted has typed Bob's email address. Recall that the term email address is used, but it is not an address; we now know that it is a domain name, a form of a network ID. Also, this "email" address might not even be for email. It might be a domain name for a Web site or for a file server. Thus, the term email address is a generic term.

Ted usually does not have to type bob.com. He may only have to paste it into a place on a mail window on the PC screen. Or, if he is looking over (say) a stock report, he may only need to click on a name to fetch another report or to be given access to another machine in the Internet. Whatever the

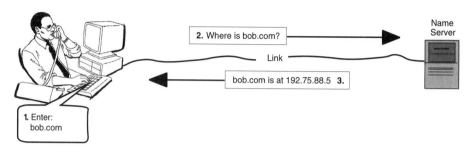

Figure 16.1   Ted Enters Bob's "Email Address"

scenarios may be, in event 1 the name is translated into an address if information is going to be routed through a network.

In event 2, the computer sends a control packet to a designated name server. This packet is coded as a name-to-address query of "Where is bob.com?" The name server receives the query and searches a table to find a record of bob.com and his associated address. In event 3, the name server finds a match and returns the answer to Ted's computer.

If the Traffic Uses a Server

You know by now that some applications using servers do not support a direct dialogue between users. Therefore, name/address resolution is to find the address of a server.

Insert the Address into the Packet

In most situations, Ted does not know that events 2 and 3 have taken place. Nor does he know about event 4, shown in Figure 16.2. A special software program in the computer places Bob's IP address in the correct field of the outgoing packet header of the email to Ted.

Figure 16.2   The Computer Takes Over

Operations at the Router

Events 5, 6, and 7 in Figure 16.3 are also invisible to Ted (and Bob). We spent quite some time on these operations in Chapter 12.

In event 5, the packet is sent to a designated router (it is set up to handle Ted's traffic). Notice that the packet contains the message. Then in event 6,

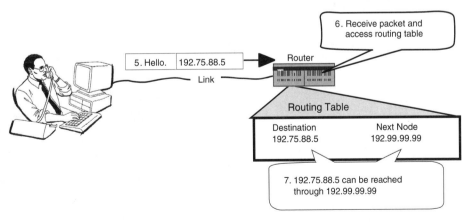

Figure 16.3   Operations at the Router

the router accepts the packet and uses the IP destination address to access the routing table. In event 7, the match of the address is found in the table, as well as the next node that is to receive the packet. This next node might even be a server.

Delivery to the Dallas Node, and Then to Chicago

In event 8, as shown in Figure 16.4, the packet is sent to the output link. It is now on its journey to the Dallas site, where the router at Dallas will forward the packet to the next node, eventually to reach Bob in Chicago. These last operations at Dallas and Chicago are simply a repeat of the steps explained in events 6, 7, and 8.

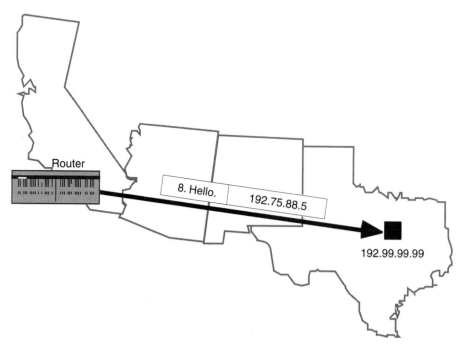

Figure 16.4 Delivery to the Dallas Node

Sending the Reply Back to Ted

Bob's reply of "OK, my name is Bob," simply reverses the process. In Figure 16.5, notice that the source and destination IP addresses and the domain names are changed in the packet and message headers, respectively. If a server is involved, the addresses are those of Bob and the server.

Although not shown in this example, the routers also have the information to forward Bob's reply back to Ted in San Diego. They have learned about this route in exactly the same manner as they learned about the route to Bob in Chicago, the subject of Chapter 13.

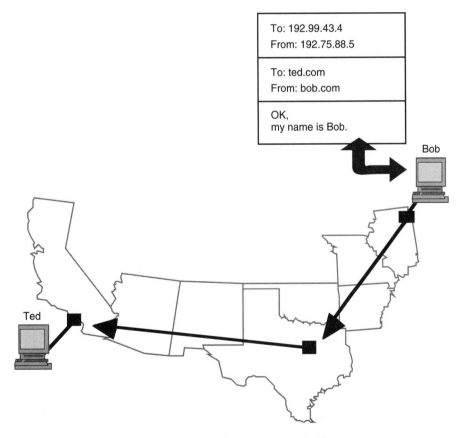

To: 192.99.43.4
From: 192.75.88.5

To: ted.com
From: bob.com

OK,
my name is Bob.

Figure 16.5   For Traffic the Other Way (No Server Involved)

Summary

Several events take place to transport information from one computer, through the Internet, to any computer in the world that has (a) an IP address and (b) an interface to the Internet.

But we now know that these supposedly simple events unfolded successfully because of a lot of operations have been taking place in the background, completely transparently to Ted and Bob. And that is one reason the Internet is so easy to use: it keeps these operations transparent to its users.

Chapter 17

Dialing in to the Net

This chapter explains the procedures for dialing in to the Internet. It discusses how the Internet Service Provider uses a customer's domain name and IP address, as well as how a customer obtains the name and address in the first place. It also explains how passwords authenticate the Internet customer.

The Dial-Up Arrangement

It has been noted in earlier chapters that there are intervening nodes, namely, the telephone office between Ted's ISP and Ted's computer. But for the ISP and Ted, it does not matter.[1] The telephone office, as well as the ISP's links to the office and the local loop to the PC, is just one logical link. The reason? When Ted logs on to his data network, he must dial the telephone number of his ISP. As shown in Figure 17.1, he is connected to this ISP and the Internet through the telephone office.

The phone number is usually entered into a file on the PC before dialing operations are invoked. When an Internet user, such as Ted, wants to use the network, he accesses this number with a click of a phone button on the PC screen and the ISP is automatically dialed by the computer.

---

1. Of course, the ISP must have agreements with the telephone company about their connection arrangements.

161

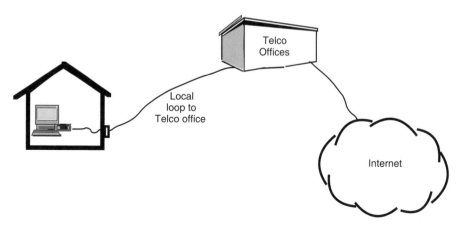

Figure 17.1   The Dial-Up Arrangement

The Dial-Up Background Hisses and Tones

If you have your PC speaker on when you are logging on to the Internet (or any data network), you will hear some pretty unusual sounds coming from your speaker. First, of course, you will hear the number of your ISP being dialed, then you will hear hisses, tones, and maybe even groans.

Some of these sounds represent special signals (frequency tones) that are being exchanged between your modem and the ISP modem, and they serve an important purpose.

You may have also noticed that your connection to the Internet might vary in the connection speed (in bits per second). Sometimes your PC screen might inform you that you are connected at 56,000 bits per second, and other times, it might read 28,800 bits per second, and so on.

Some of the tones exchanged between modems negotiate a bit rate (in bit/s) for the dial-up connection. The bit rate depends on a number of factors; those we have discussed in this book deal with the quality of the dial-in connection. If the line has a lot of noise or if the connection is poor and is leading to signal decay, the modems will agree to a lesser bit rate in order to make the bits more "robust," a subject covered in Chapter 3. This means the dial-up modems we use today are smart; for a review of this important idea, take another look at Figure 4.3 in Chapter 4.

For example, if I am dialing in to the Internet from my home (I live in the country), the poor quality of the connection usually restricts my transmission rate to a range of around 28,800 to 44,000 bits per second. If I am traveling and connect to the Internet from a hotel room, the high-quality connection usually allows me a 56,000 bits per second transmission rate.

Furnishing Information to the ISP

Figure 17.2 shows the information Internet users must furnish their ISP. In addition to the telephone number of the ISP, the Internet user must furnish at

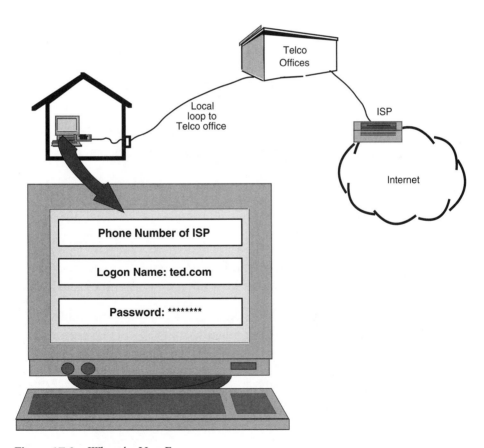

Figure 17.2 What the User Enters

163

least two other pieces of information: a domain name and a password. The question is: how does the user obtain this information in the first place?

Ted Obtains a Domain Name and an Address

The domain name can be assigned to the user by the ISP, or it can be available from organizations that are tasked with assigning domain names to the Internet community. For example, if Ted were a customer of AOL, he might be assigned the domain name of ted@aol.com. It then becomes the job of AOL to make sure its name server and other name servers (specifically, the root servers, explained in Chapter 15) know that Ted is attached to AOL's network.

As I mentioned earlier, one of my domain names is infoinst.com. This domain name is registered through an Internet registration organization, and it has nothing to do with AOL, MSN, or any other specific ISP.[2]

Furthermore, AOL usually assigns Ted an IP address. This address is taken from a pool of addresses at AOL.

In other words, Ted and Bob really don't have to do much of anything to use the invaluable IP address space and domain name space—just sign up with an ISP!

The Password

The password is a value that only Ted and his ISP know. When this password is entered at Ted's computer, it is passed to the ISP and used to make sure that Ted is really Ted; that is, that he is not an imposter trying to use Ted's account.

Typically, a password is set up between you the user and the ISP during an initial configuration; that is, when you first become a customer of the ISP. In most customer–ISP relationships, you can change the password at will.

This password is a secret password. It should not be released to those whom you do not want to log on to your Internet account.

---

2. My name is registered through Network Solutions, Inc. To find out more about obtaining a domain name, go to http://www.networksolutions.com.

The secrecy aspect of the password is the reason that it is written over by asterisks as you enter it into your computer. With this approach, someone looking over your shoulder will not be able to read it (and if you have a dual personality, you can't steal it from yourself).

The password along with your domain name (email address) allows anyone to access your account and read your email and any other information the ISP furnishes on your behalf.

What the ISP Does with the Information

The ISP uses this logon information to access special servers to authenticate Ted and also to make certain that ted.com correctly correlates to Ted's IP address. See Figure 17.3.

One of two scenarios unfolds here. First, the ISP may have Ted's address stored in one of the servers. When Ted logs on and gives the ISP his name of ted.com, the ISP is able to look up Ted's IP address. Second, as noted earlier, if Ted has not been assigned an address, the ISP will assign him one from a pool of addresses that belong to the ISP.

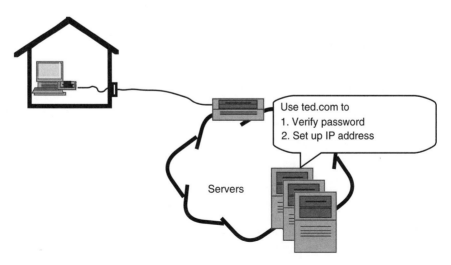

Figure 17.3 What the Network Does with Ted's Input

In the second scenario, Ted is borrowing an address from his ISP for the duration of his session. When the session is over, this address is used by another customer of this ISP. It is the job of the ISP to make sure all interested parties (namely, Bob and his ISP) know that ted.com is associated with this assigned address.

Summary

It is obvious that the Internet Service Provider does most of the work in getting a user connected to the Internet. This approach is certainly reasonable, since we are paying the ISP a fee to do just that. Nonetheless, the fact that we can dial to just about anyone in the world (who of course connects to the Internet), and exchange email, files, slides, photos, faxes, greeting cards, drawings, and so on is a remarkable service.

Chapter 18

The Web

You might be saying at this point in the book, "It's about time! Why has the author postponed any detailed reference to the Web to the back of this book?" The answer is simple: The Web operates over the Internet. It relies very heavily on IP addresses and the Domain Name System. Indeed, it cannot function without them. It was necessary to cover these subjects before discussing the Web. Therefore, if you understand how domain names function and how name servers operate, you will have an easy go of it in this chapter.

This chapter introduces the Web. Our emphasis is on the general behavior of the Web and its use of Uniform Resource Locators (URLs). We also try a couple of experiments by logging on to the Web and doing some surfing.

What the Web Does

The Web. A beguiling term. It conjures up different images from different people. Its principal inventor, Tim Berners-Lee, first came up with its ideas based upon the term *Enquire Within upon Everything*, a book that Berners-Lee remembered from his childhood.[1] As he and others developed what we call the Web, it has come to mean a way of obtaining information on the Internet.

---

1. Berners-Lee, Tim, *Weaving the Web*, Orion Publishing Group, Ltd. London WC29EA, 1999.

I also would add that often the Web provides us *Everything about Nothing*, but that is not the fault of Mr. Berners-Lee.

Anyway, the term itself is quite accurate in what it is meant to do: Allow a Web user to "glide" through internets as if the internets were intersections in a web. And at these intersections, allow the user to glide off into other intersections. What makes this idea so attractive is that these Web intersections contain information, such as news, weather, research on DNA, and on and on.

The journey through the Web can be endless. It can also be somewhat futile, depending on how we take the paths through the Web nodes.

Dependency on the DNS

For Networking 101, it is essential to know one fundamental fact about the Web: The Web is based on the Domain Name System (DNS). All of its services are tied to the ability to enter or click on a DNS name (called a URL in Web parlance) and "go to" the address of the site that is represented by the name.

To try out this idea, use the example in Figure 18.1. After you have logged on to the Internet, enter http://www.phptr.com/black on your machine (if

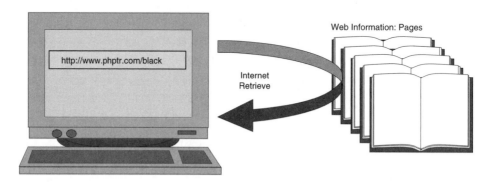

Figure 18.1 Retrieving Web Information (Note: For simplicity, you might enter only www.phptr.com/black or even phptr.com/black, depending on the system in your computer)

you do not know how to enter this name, please check your PC's user manual or your ISP user guide). You will receive back on your screen some Web "pages" (pages is another term for information).

Most likely, these pages will have my picture in them (sorry, one of the disadvantages of this specific Web retrieval) and information about some of my books and the book you are reading.

The URL

The key to the Web is the Uniform Resource Locator (URL). It was developed by Tim Berners-Lee, and he called it originally a universal document identifier. The name was changed by the Internet standards groups.

The URL is an identifier, a name. It is not an address. An IP address is still needed to route packets back and forth between the users' computers and the computers that store the pages.

A domain name may be part of the URL. For example, the URL http://www.phptr.com/black has the domain name of phptr.com in it and is used for the example in Figure 18.2. One of my domain names, infoinst.com, is part of the URL of http://www.infoinst.com. (Be aware that some systems do not require you to key in "http://"; indeed, some will not accept it.)

Here is a description of the contents of a typical URL, as depicted in Figure 18.2:

- ❐ http: The Hypertext Transfer Protocol. A protocol used to transfer Web documents. It organizes and presents Web pages (documents).

- ❐ :// and /: Delimiters in the URL. They separate the entries in the URL.

- ❐ www.phptr.com: phptr.com is the domain name of the site where the document resides. The notation of "www" refers to the Web itself.

- ❐ black: The specific document of interest.

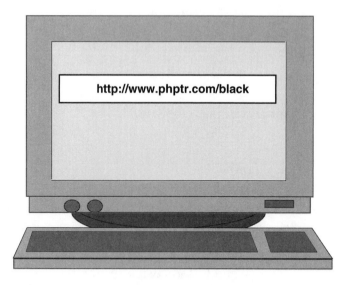

http	Hypertext Transfer Protocol
://and/	Delimiters in the URL
www.phptr.com	Domain name
black	specific document

Figure 18.2 The Web Uniform Resource Locator (URL) (Note: For some systems, simply key in www.phptr.com/black)

An Experiment: Go to http://www.infoinst.com

Let's go to the infoinst.com Web site. You retrieve a Web page from the infoinst.com site. The general flow of this operation is shown in Figure 18.3.

If you give this figure some thought, you will realize that you have already seen in this book the major operations shown in the figure with the arrow and the notation "Internet Retrieve." If your memory is a bit fuzzy, review Chapter 16, Putting It Together.

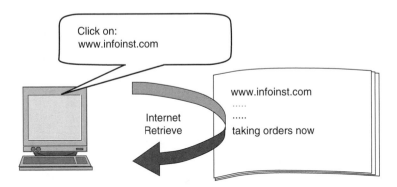

Figure 18.3 Retrieving from the infoinst.com Web Site

If You Are Interested In...

The Web software in your computer can relate some of your clicks to other URLs. For example, if you clicked on "taking orders now," this information is actually "linked" to a URL associated with the Amazon direct order company (amazon.com). This action is shown in Figure 18.4 as an "Internal Retrieve" because it does not require the sending of packets into the Internet. The information is stored in the PC's Web software and tables.

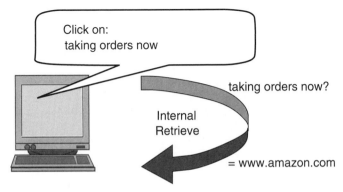

Figure 18.4 Relating the Prompt to a URL

The domain name of amazon.com is correlated to an IP address that is placed in your packet (in the IP destination address field of the header).

This packet is then routed to the amazon.com site, where its contents direct a server at the site to retrieve the information associated with the amazon.com URL.

...An Order for a Famous Book

Again, if you tried the experiment I suggested earlier, you would have retrieved a Web page from Amazon after you clicked on "taking orders now." The general flow is shown in Figure 18.5.

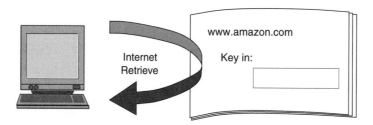

Figure 18.5   Automatic Linking to Another Web Site

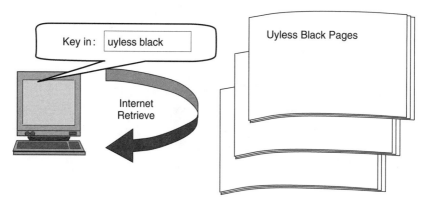

Figure 18.6   And Retrieving More Documents

Notice the entry on the Amazon page of "Key in," followed by a box; we'll use it in the next part of the experiment.

And the Next Step

If you enter uyless black inside this box, the pages associated with Uyless Black will be retrieved and sent to your computer, as shown in a general way in Figure 18.6.

Summary

We can make this summary quite succinct:

- ❒ The Web runs on the Internet.
- ❒ The Web is based on URLs.
- ❒ URLs are based on the Domain Name System (DNS).
- ❒ The DNS correlates URLs to IP addresses.
- ❒ Web links enable you to browse through the Web pages via URL, the DNS, and the IP addresses.

If this summary made any sense at all, you have just graduated from Networking 101. I trust you; just let me know that you understood it, and I'll send you a diploma. This grand diploma will gain you entry into...well, accompanied by two or three dollars, it might get you cup of coffee at the nearest coffee house.

Chapter 19

The Protocols

This chapter places some specific protocol names around many of the operations explained in this book. Some of the protocols, such as IP, have been mentioned before; others are introduced for the first time. Just a few protocols are mentioned. Communications networks and the Internet operate with scores (and even hundreds) of protocols, so we cover those that are the most prominent in a conventional Internet session.

Internet Protocol (IP)

In Chapter 12, we learned how packets are relayed in a network between users. We learned that the routers use the destination address in the packet header to determine how the packets are routed; that is, to which output link the packet is to be sent in order to reach the destination computer.

The *Internet Protocol* (IP) is essentially a forwarding protocol and is responsible for the operations explained in Chapter 12. IP carries a source IP address and a destination IP address in the IP header. The destination IP address is examined at each router and is used to access a routing table, which is then used to forward the IP packet to the next node. Figure 19.1 is a rehash of some of the operations in Chapter 12 in relation to IP.

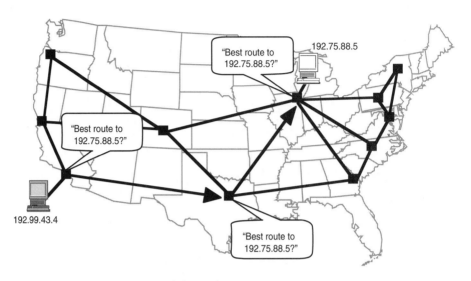

Figure 19.1 Using IP to Forward the Packet

Transmission Control Protocol (TCP)

In Chapters 2, 3, and 13, we examined the subject of acknowledging traffic. We learned in Chapter 13 that traffic acknowledgment can be performed between routers. Brief mention was made of also performing this acknowledgment between the user machines, such as the PCs that are operated by Ted and Bob. This PC-to-PC service is provided by the *Transmission Control Protocol* (TCP).

Since TCP is responsible for the reliable transfer of user traffic between two computers (in our examples, Ted's and Bob's machines or Ted's and Bob's servers), TCP uses acknowledgments (ACKs) to make certain all traffic is delivered safely to the destination endpoint. If something goes wrong and the traffic does not arrive at the receiver correctly, TCP has the means to resend the traffic. Figure 19.2 shows the operations of TCP between Ted's and Bob's computers. As before, if the traffic goes to servers, the TCP operations are between the server and the user machine.

Of course, these acknowledgment packets are being sent through the network via the San Diego, Dallas, and Chicago nodes. But the routers do not care about these "end to end" packets; their main concern is to forward them between the San Diego and Chicago users, Ted and Bob.

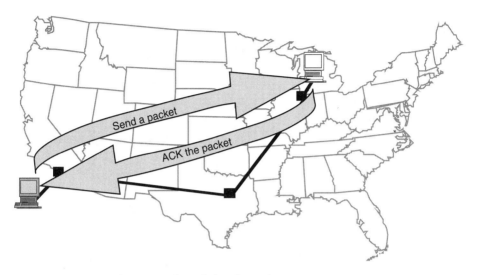

Figure 19.2   Using TCP to Acknowledge the Packet

Open Shortest Path First (OSPF)

In Chapter 13, we learned how the machines in a network learn about a route to reach a destination, such as the receiver, Bob, or Bob's server. A special control protocol was described that is executed in the routers (a) to advertise Bob's address, and (b) to select the path (or route) in the network that can be taken for a packet to reach Bob or his server. This idea is shown in Figure 19.3.

Recall that these advertisements are placed in special control packets by the advertising machine and sent to the machine's "neighbor" nodes; that is, the nodes that are directly connected to the advertising node by a communications link. In turn, these nodes then send the advertisement packets to their neighbors. Eventually, all interested nodes find out about (say) Bob's address. These operations allow each node to construct the routing table that IP uses to forward packets through the network.

Several protocols in the industry perform these services. One is called the *Open Shortest Path First* (OSPF). This protocol is used extensively throughout

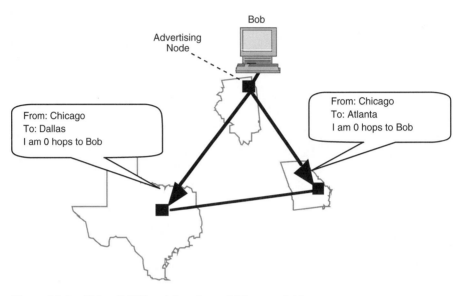

Figure 19.3 Using OSPF to Advertise and Discover Addresses

many networks (and the Internet) to advertise addresses and provide routers the information they need to build their routing tables.

Simple Mail Transfer Protocol (SMTP)

Throughout most of these chapters, examples of network traffic have focused on chat messages or email traffic. One of the Internet protocols that sends and receives email is called the *Simple Mail Transfer Protocol* (SMTP), illustrated in Figure 19.4. If you take a look at some of the text that accompanies your email message, you may come across a reference to SMTP. This reference means the email was sent via SMTP.

SMTP performs a number of services for the email users. One of the most important is that it provides a worldwide standard on how to create the email message by defining how the message is formatted. For example, the message heading, the main body of the message, etc., must be in a standard format so that any computer that receives an email message can understand its contents.

Figure 19.4 shows a generic flow, but SMTP uses mail servers as explained in scenario 4 in Appendix A.

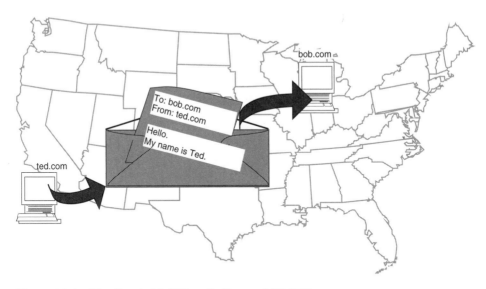

Figure 19.4 The Simple Mail Transfer Protocol (SMTP)

Hypertext Transfer Protocol (HTTP)

The *Hypertext Transfer Protocol* (HTTP), explained in Chapter 18, performs for Web pages functions similar to those that SMTP performs for email messages. See Figure 19.5. It is a worldwide standard for the transfer of Web doc-

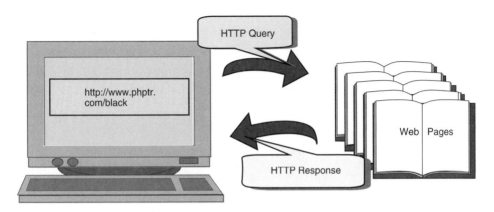

Figure 19.5 Hypertext Transfer Protocol (HTTP)

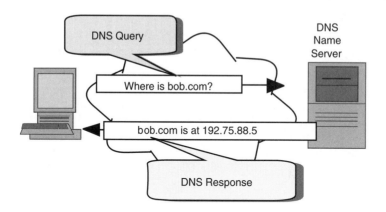

Figure 19.6 DNS and Name Servers

uments (pages). As such, it defines the procedures for exchanging Web pages, the use of URLs, and the actual syntax of the page itself.

Its value can be seen by the fact that different Web browser packages, such as Netscape Navigator and Internet Explorer, can send Web traffic between them because they are using HTTP.

Domain Name System (DNS)

DNS has been discussed extensively in this book. As Figure 19.6 depicts, DNS provides the ability to correlate domain names to addresses. You may wish to refer to Chapters 10 and 15 for a refresher on this vital protocol. Don't forget that the enquiry to the DNS name server can be performed by, say, a mail server on behalf of Ted or Bob. The operations depend on the nature of the user session, a topic explained in Appendix A.

Summary

This chapter summarized several protocols that support many of the operations explained in this book. Our approach has been to concentrate on the most basic and important Internet protocols. There are many others that you may wish to study, and references to them are provided in Chapter 20.

The Next Step

What is Next?

Puzzles come in many shapes these days, and the networking puzzle turns out to be iceberg-shaped. In *Networking 101* we have pieced together the tip of this iceberg, and now we know that many other aspects of computer networks must be added before we see the complete networking picture.

What is next? That depends on how much more you want to learn about data networks and the Internet. If you want to delve into more details about the subjects covered in this book, take a look at the next section. If you are satisfied with your knowledge of data networking in general and the Internet specifically, perhaps the next step is to simply log on to the Internet and learn more about all the wonderful sources of information available on the Web.

Follow-Ups

For more details, the next step is to read more about networks in general and the Internet specifically. I have some recommendations, and I highly recommend the following books, since I am the author of several of them.

The Advanced Communications Technology book series offers an introduction to the Internet, titled *Internet Architecture*. It would be a logical follow-up to the book you have just read. Another follow-up book is also published in this series. It is titled *Emerging Communications Technologies*. Yet another good follow-up is a book about voice over data networks. It is titled *Voice Over IP (VoIP)*.

If you want to learn more about the details of machines like modems and have a basic background in math, take a look *at The V Series Recommendations*, published by McGraw-Hill.

For the reader who is involved in software programming and/or who wants to go beyond the levels of detail in my books, I also recommend any of the Internet-oriented books written by Richard Stevens and Douglas Comer.

A Look into the Future

In a few years, the Internet of 2001 will look like a horse-and-buggy contraption. Using our computer-and-human analogy, we can say that the Internet will appear to be very intelligent and will take on characteristics of human behavior.

But as I have stated in earlier writings, we should not overestimate the ability of the upcoming network technologies, and we are very far from realizing the goal of building a computer and a computer network capable of true intellectual activity. Yet some people continue to believe computers possess rather fantastic intellectual qualities, and many articles now appear about machines that "out-think" humans.

In some tasks, computers surely do outperform humans. After all, what human can think through several hundred thousand permutations of a chess game in a few seconds? But this same machine likely cannot play checkers (well, it might if it has the appropriate software loaded); it cannot spontaneously recognize idioms and other subtleties of a human language. Indeed, there is precious little a computer can do, once we ask it to go beyond the tasks that we humans have empowered it to perform.

We should recognize that the human mind possesses some qualities that are presently undefined. Learning and cognition are largely guided by characteristics inherent in the genetic makeup of the individual, and we are just now starting to understand the human genome. Many studies indicate that intelligence is mainly innate and that much of our behavior is based on instinct. We should not expect that the computer can be designed to assume instinctual qualities, at least not until we have made the quantum leap of mapping DNA information into computer-based artificial intelligence (AI).

Presently, the computer can fool us into believing it has intelligence, but this supposed intelligence largely depends on the intelligence with which humans program the computer.

So, the sensible approach is to recognize the limits of the computer and computer networks and at the same time exploit their power to increase our productivity and enhance the quality of our lives.

We have only touched the surface of the power of computers and computer networks to bring us wealth, comfort, and joy. The computer (serving as the expert system) and the communications network (serving as the transport system) will assume a monumental role in our lives in the future. Our journey with this technology has only just begun.

And I thank you for allowing me to help you assemble the Networking 101 puzzle.

Typical User Sessions in a Computer Network

As mentioned in the preface to this book, there are a number of ways that we can obtain and exchange information in a computer network. This appendix explains them. The main body of the book uses this appendix as an anchor point for comparing and contrasting these typical user sessions in a computer network. They are described as the following scenarios:

1. Internet chat
2. Internet private messaging with a server
3. Internet private messaging directly
4. Email
5. Web browsing
6. File transfer
7. Interactive voice, video, and data dialogues with a server
8. Interactive voice and data dialogues without a server

Internet Chat

Internet chat (also called Internet relay chat) is a means for a person to communicate with a group of people in a chat room. The chatting is not with voice, but with messages typed in to the user's computer and sent to a chat room. As shown in Figure A.1, the chat room is actually a machine called an Internet relay chat server, or simply the chat server.

A person who wants to participate in a chat session connects to this server and chooses a topic (a chat room) to join. The person chooses a chat name for the session, and the server then allows this person to receive all the messages (conversations) that are taking place in the chat room. Of course, the person can also enter messages as well for the other participants to see.

Most chat rooms allow members to send sounds in their messages, and a user can instruct their computer if they wish to hear the sounds. Other options include the ability to view members as they enter (log on) and leave (log off) the room. For ease of viewing the members, the chat window on the computer screen contains the member list, which can be alphabetized with a command to the user's computer.

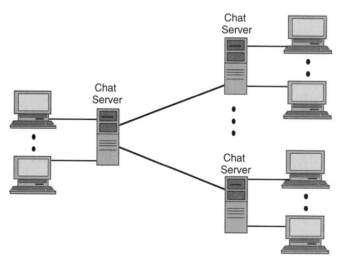

Figure A.1   Internet Chat Arrangement

Private Internet Messaging with a Server

Private Internet messaging (or simply instant messaging) is a means to "chat" with one person or a selected list of people. Unlike the public chat, a user can control who is on the chat list. Figure A.2 shows two arrangements for using instant messaging.

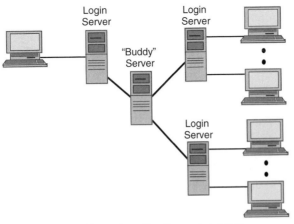

(a) Private Instant Messaging with a Server: Logging In

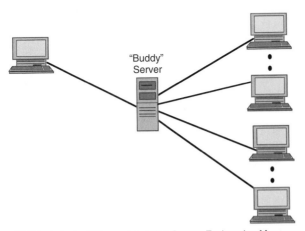

(b) Private Instant Messaging with a Server: Exchanging Messages

Figure A.2   Instant Messaging Methods

Instant messaging also uses servers. In Figure A.2(a), the user logs on to a server of the user's service provider (say, an Internet Service Provider (ISP), such as America Online). AOL performs some housekeeping activities with the user and, based on the user's input (selecting the instant messaging service icon on the computer screen), determines that the user wants to have a private chat session with any of its chat members that happen to be on-line at that time (that is, connected to the network).

In some systems (for example, AOL's Buddy List), this session is then passed to a special server called by various names (an instant messaging server, called a Buddy Server). See Figure A.2(b). The user's computer sends a buddy list to this server, based on the user selecting which set of "buddies" with whom to have chats.

If any of these chat partners are on-line (or if they come on-line), the server tells the user's computer that they are available and the user can exchange messages with them.

The buddy lists can be tailored to fit the user's preferences, such as (a) selecting a name for the chat group, (b) selecting the members for the group (using screen names of the chat members), and (c) blocking the sending to and receiving from certain members for privacy (that is, having private or public chats within the group itself).

Private Instant Messaging Directly

Some systems require these chat messages to go through the server. Others, once users are logged on, allow the messages to flow back and forth directly between the users.

Email

The main difference between public/private chat sessions and email is that email does not require the users to be logged on to the network to receive messages. As shown in Figure A.3, the email message is stored at a mail server and can be retrieved at any time by the email recipient. This means the message is not sent directly to a person's computer, but to a designated mail server for the user.

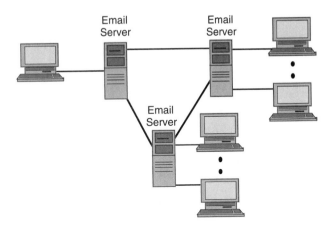

Figure A.3   The Email Arrangement

Web Browsing

Web browsing also entails the user of a server. But the Web browser is software that runs on the user's computer. It communicates with the Web servers. As shown in Figure A.4, a user gains access to the Web (this topic is explained in more detail in Chapter 18) by typing in or clicking on a special identifier called a Uniform Resource Locator (URL; explained in Chapter 18). For this discussion, the URL is the ID of a Web server that the user wants to visit; that is, a Web site. This ID is sufficient for the network to find the appropriate Web server and send the user's message to this server. The message is usually a Web query, one that asks the server to return information to the user. And this

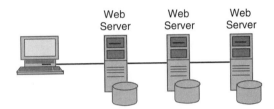

Figure A.4   The Web Browsing Arrangement

information can be almost anything: text, graphics, video images, photographs, voice, and so on.

The Web architecture also allows a user to access more than one Web server. This operation is accomplished by a user selecting additional URLs that are displayed on the user's computer screen. In this manner, the Web servers can be "linked" together to provide the needed information to the user.

File Transfer

File transfer is a popular means of exchanging information in a computer network. In contrast to the previous scenarios, file transfer usually entails the exchange of large amounts of data, but it also entails the use of a server, as shown in Figure A.5. The user's computer runs client software, and the file transfer servers run the server software. The File Transfer Protocol (FTP) is a popular file transfer protocol.

When users log on to an FTP site, they can usually browse through a list of available files that can be downloaded to their computer. FTP allows a service, called anonymous FTP, which allows anyone to access the server and download the files. Other FTP implementations are more restrictive and require passwords or other forms of authentication.

FTP is a bit different from the other scenarios described thus far in that it uses two different sessions to transfer files. One session is used for sending control messages back and forth between the client and the server. The other is used for the actual transfer of the files.

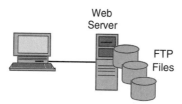

Figure A.5 The File Transfer Arrangement

Interactive Voice, Video, and Data Dialogues With a Server

A newcomer to the user sessions scenario is the ability to send and receive instant voice, video, and data traffic, all in one integrated session. So, we can't really say this scenario is typical. The concept is shown in Figure A.6. The user computer now has audio and video facilities, in addition to its data capabilities. It also uses a server (although systems are under development that allow users to communicate directly with each other).

This example shows a video conference. A conference moderator at site A is speaking into a video camera and an accompanying microphone. At the same time, the speaker can be sending data, drawing pictures, downloading a spread sheet—almost anything, depending on the nature of the session. This traffic is sent to a server. At this server is a distribution list of users that are to receive the information. The server then sends out the traffic to this list of users (a concept called multicasting).

All participants in this conference often are able to communicate back to the moderator or with each other. Under the control of the moderator, a user can be "granted" the microphone and speak to the moderator and the other members of the conference. In some implementations, video is provided only at the moderator's site, but nothing precludes having video at each site.

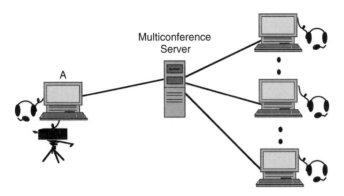

Figure A.6　Voice, Video, Data Arrangement

This scenario is technically possible and partially made possible with all-digital techniques, a subject covered in Chapter 5. Integrated voice, video, and data will become a popular means of communications in the near future. What is needed is sufficient bandwidth to support this application, a topic explained in Chapter 6.

Interactive Voice and Data Dialogues without a Server

For this service, the setup in Figure A.6 applies, sans the server. In other words, the user machines communicate directly with each other. This approach will gain popularity because it provides considerably more flexibility by not having to subscribe to a server. As an example, IBM and Microsoft support a widely used conferencing protocol, named H.323, that supports this service as one of its options.

Modulation Techniques

To use the analog signal for data transmission (digital transmission), the industry developed a clever and relatively simple device called a modem. The term is a derivative of the words *mod*ulator and *dem*odulator.

Three basic methods of digital-to-analog modulation are employed by a modem, as shown in Figure B.1. Some modems use more than one of the methods. Each method impresses the data on an analog *carrier* signal, which is altered to carry the properties of the digital data stream. The three methods are called amplitude modulation, frequency modulation, and phase modulation.

- ❏ Amplitude modulation alters the amplitude of the signal in accordance with the digital bit stream. This technique is described in the main body of this book.

- ❏ Frequency modulation alters the frequency of the signal in accordance with the digital bit stream. The frequency of a signal defines how many cycles per second the signal uses; recall that we examined this idea in Chapter 3. It is an easy process: the frequency of the signal is simply shifted up or down to represent 1s and 0s.

❐ Phase modulation alters the phase of the signal in accordance with the digital bit stream. This idea is a bit more complex. A phase is a specific point in a signal's cycle. In the figure, the cycle of the analog signal has been changed; it was not allowed to "cycle over" to a positive voltage but was returned immediately to a negative voltage. Thus, its phase was shifted, and when the shift occurred, a 1 was represented. If a "no shift" occurs during a sampled time, then a 0 is represented.

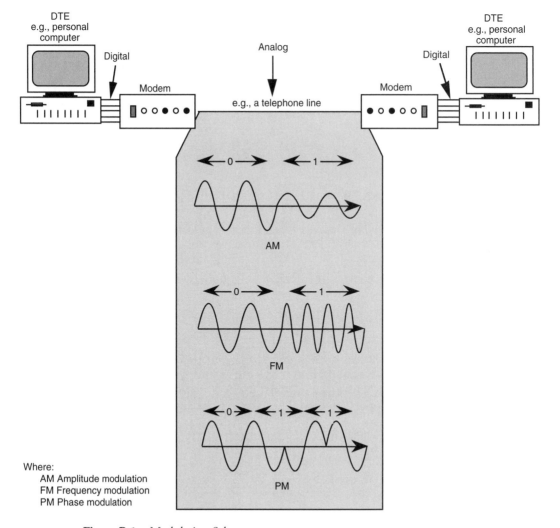

Figure B.1   Modulation Schemes

Appendix C

Codes

Codes are the "language" used by the machines to direct their actions. The codes are based on binary numbers. Most of us are familiar with the decimal number system, consisting of the numbers 0–9. However, machines and the interconnecting channels are designed to support only two signal states: 0 or 1. For example, the binary equivalent of 394 is 110001010. Its decimal value can be established through positional notation:

$$
\begin{array}{ccccccccccccccccc}
& 1\mathrm{x}2^8 & + & 1\mathrm{x}2^7 & + & 0\mathrm{x}2^6 & + & 0\mathrm{x}2^5 & + & 0\mathrm{x}2^4 & + & 1\mathrm{x}2^3 & + & 0\mathrm{x}2^2 & + & 1\mathrm{x}2^1 & + & 0\mathrm{x}2^0 \\
\text{or} & 1 & + & 1 & + & 0 & + & 0 & + & 0 & + & 1 & + & 0 & + & 1 & + & 0 \\
\text{or} & 256 & + & 128 & + & 0 & + & 0 & + & 0 & + & 8 & + & 0 & + & 2 & + & 0 \\
\text{or} & 394_{10} & & & & & & & & & & & & & & & &
\end{array}
$$

Each binary digit is called a *bit*. A group of eight bits makes up a byte or octet (although in some systems seven bits make up a byte).

Binary numbers and codes are represented by several signaling techniques. A system can represent data by simply switching a current on or off, by changing the direction of current flow, or by measuring a current and its associated electromagnetic field. It is also possible to measure the voltage state of the line (such as on/off voltage, or positive or negative voltage) to represent binary 1s and 0s. Increasingly, optical fiber systems are used to transmit light pulses to represent binary 1s and 0s.

The ASCII code is a seven-bit code, although many vendors add an eighth bit for error checking. This bit is called a *parity bit*. The ASCII code is an international standard; it conforms to the International Alphabet 5 or IA5. It is the favored code by most communications vendors. Figure C.1 shows bit combinations used for this code.

Bit Positions				7 0	0	0	0	1	1	1	1
				6 0	0	1	1	0	0	1	1
4	3	2	1	5 0	1	0	1	0	1	0	1
0	0	0	0	NUL	DLE	SP	0	@	P	\	p
0	0	0	1	SOH	DC1	!	1	A	Q	a	q
0	0	1	0	STX	DC2	"	2	B	R	b	r
0	0	1	1	ETX	DC3	#	3	C	S	c	s
0	1	0	0	EOT	DC4	$	4	D	T	d	t
0	1	0	1	ENQ	NAK	%	5	E	U	e	u
0	1	1	0	ACK	SYN	&	6	F	V	f	v
0	1	1	1	BEL	ETB	'	7	G	W	g	w
1	0	0	0	BS	CAN	(	8	H	X	h	x
1	0	0	1	HT	EM	)	9	I	Y	i	y
1	0	1	0	LF	SUB	*	:	J	Z	j	z
1	0	1	1	VT	ESQ	+	;	K	[	k	{
1	1	0	0	FF	FS	'	<	L	\	l	:
1	1	0	1	CR	GS	-	=	M	]	m	}
1	1	1	0	SO	RS	.	>	N	^	n	~
1	1	1	1	SI	US	/	?	O	-	o	DEL

Figure C.1 The ASCII/IA5 Code

Index

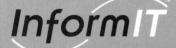